TWAYNE'S WORLD AUTHORS SERIES

A Survey of the World's Literature

Sylvia E. Bowman, Indiana University

GENERAL EDITOR

RUSSIA

N. P. Vaslef, U. S. Air Force Academy

EDITOR

A. K. Tolstoy

(TWAS 168)

TWAYNE'S WORLD AUTHORS SERIES (TWAS)

The purpose of TWAS is to survey the major writers —novelists, dramatists, historians, poets, philosophers, and critics—of the nations of the world. Among the national literatures covered are those of Australia, Canada, China, Eastern Europe, France, Germany, Greece, India, Italy, Japan, Latin America, New Zealand, Poland, Russia, Scandinavia, Spain, and the African nations, as well as Hebrew, Yiddish, and Latin Classical literatures. This survey is complemented by Twayne's United States Authors Series and English Authors Series.

The intent of each volume in these series is to present a critical-analytical study of the works of the writer; to include biographical and historical material that may be necessary for understanding, appreciation, and critical appraisal of the writer; and to present all material in clear, concise English—but not to vitiate the scholarly content of the work by doing so.

A. K. Tolstoy

By MARGARET DALTON

Twayne Publishers, Inc. :: New York

Preface

Russian nineteenth-century literature outside of Russia is primarily known for its prose. Yet the nineteenth century was equally important in poetry. The Golden Age of Russian poetry during the first three decades of the century yielded all the classics of Russian verse: Zhukovsky, Batyushkov, Pushkin, Baratynsky, Tyutchev, Lermontov. The end of the nineteenth century brought with it a renaissance of poetry under the influence of European Symbolism known as the Silver Age of Russian poetry, the principal representatives of which included Bryusov, Balmont, Sologub, Gippius, Annensky, Bely, and Blok. Even the middle of the nineteenth century which saw the appearance of the most outstanding Russian novelists—Dostoevsky, Goncharov, Turgenev, Leo Tolstoy—was not only a period of prose. Poetry continued to be written, although its position had become a rather precarious "coexistence." The primary reason for this lay in the attitude of radical literary critics—extremely influential and vocal in Russia—who following the dictum of their *maître* Vissarion Belinsky, demanded that art reflect the "burning issues" of the day and be inspired by socially significant ideas.

Whereas many—although by no means, all—prose works permitted a variety of interpretations, including a "social" one, poetry was less tractable in this respect. There were, of course, poets who wrote about social ills (serfdom, poverty, injustice, etc.), but, with the exception of Nikolay Nekrasov, whose talent outweighed his "civic" ideology, few of them are remembered today. It is rather those poets who adhered to the theory of "pure art"—art freely created and not tied to any specific ideology or purpose—who kept the fires of poetry burning during that period. Although few in number, misunderstood, and sometimes virtually silenced (e.g., Afanasy Fet), they have subsequently found their well-deserved places in Russian literary history. In a sense, these poets may be regarded as connecting links between the Golden Age and the Silver Age of Russian poetry. One such poet was A. K. Tolstoy.

Among the poets of his generation, A. K. Tolstoy was the most versatile, original, and ultimately the most interesting. He started as a prose writer, probably following the trend of the time, but dropped this medium after having written several short stories and a full-length novel. Poetry was his real vocation, one in which he could exhibit best his creative energies and diversity, and there is virtually no poetic form which he did not use at some period of his life. To the early period—the 1840's and 1850's—belong his shorter poems: lyric poetry, imitation of folk songs, translations, humorous poems and ballads. In his mature period, from the late 1850's on, Tolstoy turned to longer forms, narratives-in-verse and drama. His historical trilogy, *The Death of Ivan the Terrible, Czar Fyodor,* and *Czar Boris,* written in the 1860's, belongs to the outstanding dramatic works of Russian nineteenth-century literature.

The first complete edition of Tolstoy's works was issued in 1882, seven years after the poet's death, for it was only toward the end of the nineteenth and the beginning of the twentieth centuries that interest in him was revived. Articles on various aspects of the poet's work by eminent writers and critics began to appear. The philosopher and poet Vladimir Solovyov, closely connected with the Symbolist movement, rediscovered Tolstoy together with other neglected poets. Tolstoy's tragedies, which had previously suffered many vicissitudes, were staged at the Moscow Art Theater where they enjoyed tremendous success; new translations of Tolstoy's novel *Prince Serebryany,* and his tragedies, and the dramatic poem *Don Juan* appeared in French, German, and English.

A massive monograph on Tolstoy's life and work by André Lirondelle in French was published in 1912. Since that time, however, no new study of the poet has appeared. Soviet scholarship in general tended to overlook Tolstoy for ideological reasons, for his esthetic views, his opposition to the radicals, and his monarchist sympathies made it difficult to fit him into the prescribed norm. It is only recently (1963) that Tolstoy's works have been reissued in the Soviet Union. Western scholars, on the other hand, were inclined to concentrate on the "giants" of Russian literature or on contemporary Soviet literature, leaving many interesting poets and writers of the nineteenth century unexamined.

The present study of A. K. Tolstoy is an attempt to fill the void surrounding "secondary" figures in Russian literature. Its objective is to provide an introduction to the poet for the general reader, and to give a concise reference work to the student of Russian literature. By necessity, the scope of the study is limited, and is general rather than detailed. A more specialized study of Tolstoy's poetry is, no doubt, needed and will be welcomed by scholars in the field. However, within the prevailing limits the author has tried to discuss most of the characteristic and important works of the poet, and to give a general idea of the times in which he lived.

Contents

Chronology

1817   August 24. Count Alexey Konstantinovich Tolstoy born in St. Petersburg.

1817-   Childhood in the Ukraine.
1826

1827   First trip abroad (Karlsbad, Dresden, Weimar).

1831   Second trip abroad (Italy).

1834   Begins work at Moscow Archives of the Ministry of Foreign Affairs.

1835   Receives University diploma.

late   Attached to the Russian Embassy in Frankfurt am Main,
1830's Germany; trips to Italy, France.

1840   Returns to St. Petersburg; appointed to Second Section of Imperial Chancellery.

1841   First story, "The Vampire," published.

1843   First poem published.

1840's A number of poems and stories written, but not published; steady advancement at Imperial Court.

1850-   Meeting with Sofya Andreevna Miller, later to become Tol-
1851   stoy's wife.

1851   Appointed Master of Ceremonies at Imperial Court.

1854   Poetry printed in *The Contemporary*; beginning of literary career.

1855-   Participates in Crimean War.
1856

1856   Appointed aide-de-camp of Czar Alexander II.

1850's High point of lyric production.

1858   Narrative-in-verse, *The Sinner*.

1859   Narrative-in-verse, *John Damascenus*.

1861   Resigns from post at Imperial Court.

1862   Publication of Dramatic Poem, *Don Juan,* and Historical Novel, *Prince Serebryany*.

1863   Marriage to Sofya Andreevna Miller.

1866   Tragedy, *The Death of Ivan the Terrible*.

1867   *The Death of Ivan the Terrible* staged in St. Petersburg. Only lifetime edition of Tolstoy's poetry.

1868   *The Death of Ivan the Terrible* staged in Weimar. Tragedy, *Czar Fyodor*.

late "Norman-Russian" ballads and poetry written.
1860's

1870 Tragedy, *Czar Boris*.

1874 Narrative-in-verse. *The Portrait* and satiric poem, "The Dream of Popov."

1875 Narrative-in-verse, *The Dragon*.

1875 September 28: died at Krasny Rog.

CHAPTER 1

Life

I *Family Background*

O N November 13, 1816 the marriage of Count Konstantin Petrovich Tolstoy to Anna Alexeevna Perovskaya took place in St. Petersburg. Among the family members attending the ceremony were Count Peter Tolstoy, the father of the groom, Count Alexey Razumovsky, the father of the bride, and Alexey Perovsky, her brother. The match was unequal in many ways, proved to be short-lived, and subsequently gave rise to persistent rumors of scandal.

Count Konstantin Petrovich belonged to an old, but impoverished, noble family.[1] His father, Peter Petrovich Tolstoy, was a military man (he eventually reached the rank of major general) with a reputation for sterling honesty and material disinterestedness which kept him constantly on the edge of poverty. Konstantin Petrovich, born in 1780 as one of thirteen children, received the usual education of a noble in the Cadet Corps. At the age of seventeen he was made an officer, and took part in the Swedish and French campaigns in which he was wounded and decorated for bravery. However, army life apparently did not appeal to him, for he retired from it at the age of twenty-six, with the rank of colonel. His subsequent career was undistinguished and included service in the Senate and at the State Bank in St. Petersburg. Konstantin Petrovich's appearance and personality were also in no way outstanding. "He was not handsome, but had an extremely kind . . . face," his niece recalled; although strong in body, he was "hasty and awkward in his movements."[2] Lacking ambition or talent, he was gay, weak of character, and given to drink. Having become a widower after a brief marriage, he contracted a second marriage with the seventeen-year-old Anna Alexeevna Perovskaya.

The Perovskys by far outshone the Tolstoys in prominence and wealth, although their nobility was of a more recent date: it

13

originated from the elevation of a Ukrainian Cossack, Alexey
Razum, to the position of Empress Elizabeth's morganatic husband. Count Alexey Kirillovich Razumovsky, the nephew of
Alexey Razum, served as senator under Catherine the Great and
as minister of public education under Alexander I. For many
years the Count kept up a *liaison* with Maria Mikhaylovna Sobol-
evskaya by whom he had nine children. These children were
legitimized by an Imperial order under the name of Perovsky.
One of them, born in 1799, was Anna Alexeevna who became
the poet's mother.

Relatively little is known of Anna Alexeevna's early life. It can
be assumed, however, that she received a good education and
that she grew up in an atmosphere of leisure and wealth. A portrait painted of her by the French painter, Madame Vigée-
Lebrun, shows Anna Alexeevna as a "beautiful brunette with a
matte teint and grey eyes."[3] According to family tradition she
was intelligent and extremely headstrong and domineering. Her
marriage to Konstantin Petrovich—nearly twenty years her senior
and no match for her intellect and will—may have been an act of
self-assertion or of desperation. On August 24, 1817 Anna Alexeevna gave birth to a son, Alexey, in St. Petersburg. Six weeks
later she left her husband for good, and took her son to the
Ukraine where the Perovsky estates were located. Alexey Tolstoy spent his childhood on the estates of his mother and of his
maternal uncle, Alexey Perovsky.

Anna Alexeevna's sudden and unexplained separation from her
husband, the rupture of her hitherto friendly relations with the
Tolstoys,[4] and especially her close relation with her brother (who
remained unmarried all his life) soon gave rise to piquant rumors. It was suggested that Alexey Tolstoy was the child of an
incestuous union between Perovsky and his sister, and that the
marriage to Tolstoy had been arranged to cover up a scandal.[5]
Although the "incest theory" has been rejected by some biog-
raphers of Tolstoy,[6] and although it is contradicted by the official records of Anna Alexeevna's marriage and her son's birth,
it was repeated throughout Alexey Tolstoy's life and even after
his death. Since the parties involved never made any unequivocal
statement on this matter, Tolstoy's real origin will remain a mystery. In any case Perovsky took the place of a father in Tolstoy's

life, and did more for him than Konstantin Petrovich could have done. For not only did he lavish love and affection upon the boy, but he also carefully supervised his education, awakened his literary and artistic interests, and was his main guide and adviser during the first nineteen years of Tolstoy's life.

Alexey Alexeevich Perovsky (known in literature under the *nom de plume* of Antony Pogorelsky) belonged to the aristocratic and intellectual elite of his time. After having obtained a doctorate in philosophy and literature at the University of Moscow in 1807, he divided his time between public service, literary work, travel, and art collecting. His official career, which apparently did not interest him much, included service in the Senate, in the Department for Spiritual Affairs of Foreign Confessions, (*Departament dukhovnykh del inostrannykh ispovedanii*, a supervisory office for all non-Orthodox denominations), and as curator of Kharkov University. His interest in literature was genuine and lasting. Before the Napoleonic War he had already mingled in literary circles and was well acquainted with Karamzin, A. I. Turgenev, Vyazemsky, and Zhukovsky. During the Napoleonic War, Perovsky was stationed at Dresden, at that time one of the cultural centers of Europe.[7] Returning to Russia, Perovsky renewed his literary connections which came to include Pushkin and poets of his "Pleiad," and took a lively part in the literary debates of the time. In the late 1820's he wrote a number of stories which enjoyed considerable success among the public, as well as among men of letters. Pushkin was enchanted with one of Perovsky's Romantic tales, while Vyazemsky called him "our genuine, only novelist."[8] Perovsky's election to the Russian Academy in 1829 was a clear indication of his prominence in the world of letters. Although literature was Perovsky's great love, he was also vividly interested in the arts. During his travels in Europe in the late 1820's and early 1830's, Perovsky visited famous art galleries, bought antiques, and met with prominent painters and sculptors. His art collection seems to have been impressive and included works by Titian.

II *Childhood*

Tolstoy's early childhood was spent in the Ukrainian countryside on Perovsky's estate, Pogoreltsy, and later on his mother's estate at Krasny Rog. His memories of this period were very happy: he was surrounded by the loving care of his mother and Perovsky, and an atmosphere of luxury and refinement. The beauty of the South Russian landscape instilled in him a deep and lasting love of nature and country life. "I spent all my childhood in the woods," Tolstoy reminisced many years later.[9] The house in Krasny Rog, built by the famous Italian architect Rastrelli, remained Tolstoy's favorite residence in his later years. The abundance of impressions, a strong imagination, and the presence of an extensive library turned Tolstoy toward poetry at an early age. In his autobiographical sketch he says:

"From the age of six I began . . . to write poetry, so impressed was my imagination by the works of our best poets which I found in some thick anthology. . . . I was intoxicated by the music of various rhythms and adopted their technique. No matter how absurd my first experiments were, I must say that in regard to metrics they were irreproachable."[10]

The idyllic life in the country ended in 1826 when Perovsky was appointed to a committee on educational matters, and was forced to take up residence in St. Petersburg. Anna Alexeevna with her son followed him there. Through the poet Zhukovsky, a friend of the Perovskys, Alexey Tolstoy was presented to the heir-apparent (the future Czar Alexander II) who, like Tolstoy, was then eight years old. Tolstoy became a member of the select circle of Alexander's playmates—an honor which was conferred on only a few. However, this early tie with Alexander and the Imperial Court was to develop into "golden chains" which bore heavily on Tolstoy in his later years. A contemporary who saw Tolstoy as a boy at Court, noted his vitality and strength—he even once challenged Czar Nicholas I to fight with him—as well as his prodigious memory.[11] Although the family stayed now mainly in the capital or in Moscow, they also undertook two trips abroad, one of which proved of great importance to the young boy.

The first trip in 1827 took the travelers to Karlsbad, Dresden, and Weimar. At Weimar, Alexey Tolsoy played with the future grand duke, Carl Alexander, and studied German with a tutor. He also accompanied Perovsky on a visit to the aging Goethe who received his visitors kindly and whose "majestic features" impresssed themselves upon the boy's memory. But it was the second trip, to Italy in 1831, which left a lasting imprint on the future poet. More than twenty years later Tolstoy still spoke of it as "the artistic epoch" of lis life, as his "sixteenth century" when all his "thoughts and feelings were concentrated on love of art."[12] And in his autobiography written shortly before his death Tolstoy spoke again of the powerful impression which the art treasures of Italy had on his youthful imagination and the development of his character.

The travelers spent over two months in Italy, visiting Venice, Verona, Milan, Genoa, Florence, Rome, and Naples. In each of the cities they went to see famous historical sights, museums, and art galleries. Tolstoy's diary of the trip—naïve but charming in its earnest intent at recording all impressions—shows considerable knowledge of Roman history and mythology, familiarity with famous artists and their works, as well as an artistic sensitivity which is remarkable in a boy of thirteen. Thus, Tolstoy ventures some criticism on Thorwaldsen's famous sculpture of Christ, in which he finds "too little facial expression"; he is delighted with some marble bas-relief in a church in Florence and mentions the excellence of its composition and drawing. In Venice he is infatuated with the bust of a faun attributed to Michelangelo: "I have never seen so much expression in a marble bust; he laughs and forces you to laugh," he records in his diary. When Perovsky bought the bust and it was delivered to their hotel, the boy's happiness knew no bounds: "I lay near it for hours, I tried to lift it, I wanted to know whether I could save it in case of fire; as soon as I would have a free moment I would run to [see] it. . . . I could not believe in my happiness," Tolstoy recalls in a letter.[13] This infatuation with beauty found artistic re-creation in Tolstoy's late narrative in verse, *The Portrait*.

After returning to Russia, Tolstoy for a long time was inconsolable—suffering from acute *"Heimweh"* for his lost paradise—to the point where he even refused food and drink. But life in Moscow where Perovsky had taken up residence since his resignation from official duties had also its charms. Poets, painters, and *litterateurs* were frequent visitors in Perovsky's house. Tolstoy even caught a glimpse of Pushkin who came to see Perovsky, and Pushkin is also supposed to have approved of some of Tolstoy's juvenile poems which Perovsky showed him.

III *Education and Career*

Tolstoy's education so far had been conducted at home, as was the custom among aristocratic families, but the tradition of service to the state soon forced Anna Alexeevna and Perovsky to choose a career for the boy. After some deliberation, military service was discarded in favor of government service, and in 1834, at sixteen, Tolstoy began work at the Moscow Archives of the Ministry of Foreign Affairs as a "student." At the same time Tolstoy was being tutored by professors of Moscow University with the view of obtaining a university diploma. This connection with the Archives and with Moscow University, even thought short-lived, had some influence on Tolstoy's intellectual development, for although the generation of "Wisdom-lovers" *Liubomudry* (Russian translation of the Greek word *philosophoi*; a group of Russian adherents of German Idealist philosophers) had left it, both the University and the Archives were still centers of intellectual fermentation and study of German Idealist philosophy. Tolstoy's teachers are not known by name, yet it seems probable that he was exposed to the ideas of such Schellingians as Professors Nadezhdin and Pavlov. At any rate, German Idealism became one of the basic philosophic systems of Tolstoy's life. Simultaneously, the Archives fostered Tolstoy's interest in history, since one of the duties of the "Archive-youths" was the selection and description of ancient documents. This interest was to manifest itself soon in Tolstoy's literary work. In the fall of 1835 Tolstoy passed the university examination and received a diploma which gave him the right to serve in the government as an official of the first rank.

Bryullov's portrait of Tolstoy painted at that time presents an extremely handsome youth with large blue eyes, blond hair, and a noble, aristocratic bearing. Prince Alexander Vasilevich Meshchersky, a close friend of Tolstoy at that period, complemented this image in his Memoirs: "Never in my life have I seen in a man such a clear and candid soul, such a responsive and tender heart, such an everpresent . . . high moral ideal as in Tolstoy."[14]

The Moscow period was soon to come to an end. In the summer of 1836 Tolstoy obtained leave of absence from the Archives in order to accompany the ailing Perovsky on a trip abroad. But the travelers got only as far as Warsaw, where Perovsky died in the arms of his nephew to whom he left his fortune. Perovsky's early death—he was only forty-nine—was a heavy blow to Tolstoy.

He did not return to Moscow to resume his work, but went to St. Petersburg with his mother. From then on, he became more and more closely connected with the life of official St. Petersburg. In view of the difference of intellectual climates in the two cities, this is of some significance.

The late 1830's were Tolstoy's *Wanderjahre*: After a short period of service with the Department of Economic Affairs in St. Petersburg, Tolstoy was attached to the Russian Embassy at the German Diet in Frankfurt. It was there that he made the acquaintance of Gogol who was visiting Zhukovsky. Tolstoy's duties at the Embassy were apparently not too taxing. In 1838 he accompanied Zhukovsky and the heir-apparent to Italy. Echoes of this second Italian trip are to be found in Tolstoy's early story, "The Vampire." In 1839 Tolstoy undertook a trip to Paris, and in 1840 he returned to Russia after an absence of nearly three years.

An appointment to the Second Section of the Imperial Chancellery awaited him in St. Petersburg. He took up residence with his mother who watched jealously over his activities, and tried to further his career. A romance with the sister of his friend, Meshchersky, was vetoed by Anna Alexeevna for unknown reasons. Tolstoy submitted to his mother's wishes without great struggle and the early poem "Farewell," in which the poet takes leave of the beloved in the hope of meeting in the other world, may have been inspired by this frustrated love experience.

There is little information on Tolstoy's life in the 1840's. His official career at Court proceded smoothly. In 1842 he was named "Titular Councillor" and in 1843 "Gentleman of the Chamber of His Majesty." In 1845 he was appointed "Collegiate Assessor" and a year later, "Councillor of the Court." These duties did not interfere with a prolonged trip abroad (in 1846/ 47), or with an active social life. According to the testimony of a contemporary,[15] Tolstoy in the 1840's led the typical life of society youth, dancing, flirting and hunting—the latter becoming a real "passion" for a while. His success in society was aided by his extraordinary good looks which were combined with great physical strength: he could drive nails into a wall with his bare hands, straighten horse shoes, and bend poking irons. His penchant for humor manifested itself in the many pranks played by him and his cousins, the Zhemchuzhnikovs, which were known in all St. Petersburg. For example, one night they awakened the most famous architects in St. Petersburg, telling them that the Cathedral of St. Isaaky had collapsed and ordering them to report to the palace, which they dutifully did—to the great annoyance of Czar Nicholas I.[16] At the same time, there was another side to Tolstoy's nature which found pleasure in solitary musing, reading, and writing.

The 1840's have been termed "the most important epoch in the spiritual life of post-Petrine Russia," when "philosophical interests spread with the persistence and quickness of a psychic infection."[17] Earlier enthusiasm for Schelling and Fichte was giving way to infatuation with Hegel: "Hegelianism was the basis of everything: it was floating in the air, and was being expressed in newspaper and journal articles, in stories, in treatises, in art, in sermons, in conversation. A person who did not know Hegel had no right to speak: he who wanted to know the truth studied Hegel. Everything was based on it. . . ."[18] One of the "practical" outgrowths of this intellectual fermentation was the division of Russian society into Slavophiles and Westernizers and another was the growth of Russian socialism, based on the writings on Saint-Simon and Fourier. Literature, too, underwent significant changes. The decline of poetry which had started in the 1830's, led to the growing ascendance of prose which was quite distinct from that of the previous decade. "The Romantic cult of pure art became noticeably weaker, while a . . . Realistic manner, with social tendencies, became stronger."[19] Vissarion Belinsky's socially oriented literary criticism, which gave its coloring to nearly the whole century, was also an important feature of the 1840's.

It seems probable that Tolstoy remained at a certain distance from the intellectual and social debates of that period which were fought primarily in Moscow. His duties at the Court connected him with the conservative elements in St. Petersburg, while his social life revolved around the aristocratic *salons* of Vladimir Odoevsky, Sollogub, and others. It was through his aristocratic connections that Tolstoy ventured into literature. He showed some of his youthful poems to Odoevsky whose Romantic philosophical and literary views must have appealed to him. At Sollogub's *salon* he read his story "The Vampire." To professional men of letters it must have smacked of dilettantism. The poet and critic P. Pletnev wrote in a letter to a friend: "I went to a 'soirée' at Sollogubs; there I found a large gathering composed of aristocratic *littérateurs* and most charming ladies. Zhukovsky, Odoevsky, and many others were there. The reading of a story by Count Tolstoy took place—a young man whose mother is a née Perovskaya. The story is called 'The Vampire.' I do not like this type, and I especially don't like *salon* readings."[20] In May, 1841, Tolstoy submitted the story with a respectful letter to the censor, A. V. Nikitenko: "I do not think that it contains anything contrary to the laws of censorship," the young author wrote, and expressed the hope that no revision would be required.[21] Soon thereafter the story was published in a limited edition under the pseudonym, "Krasnorogsky."[22]

Despite the fact that Tolstoy made his literary debut in prose, the spirit of his story was by no mean Realistic, but went back to the tradition of Romantic literature, especially the Gothic horror tales which were Tolstoy's favorite reading material at the time. This fact accounted for the negative reception which was accorded to "The Vampire" upon its publication. The Petersburg journals, such as *Son of the Fatherland* (*Syn otechestva*), *The Northern Bee* (*Severnaia pchela*) and *Library for Reading* (*Biblioteka dlia chteniia*) gave it sarcastic reviews, attributing it, among other things, to the author's "over-indulgence in opium."[23] Only Belinsky reviewed it more favorably, but more for the potential talent of the author than for the story as such, which was too fantastic for his taste. Otherwise, "The Vampire" caused no stir in the world of letters, and probably because of its poor reception, Tolstoy did not attempt to publish two other fantastic tales, written at about the same time in French. "La famille du Vourdalak" was translated by Markevich in 1884, while "Le rendez-vous dans trois cents ans" was first printed in 1912.

In the following years Tolstoy turned to a more Realistic style. An account of a visit to the Orenburg area appeared under the title "Two Days in the Kirghiz Steppe" ("Dva dnia v kirgizskoi stepi"). A fragment, "A Wolf's Fosterchild" ("Volchii priemysh") was printed in 1843. The short story "Artemy Semyonovich Bervenkovsky" was published in 1845. The idea for a fantastic novel with the title *Stebelkovsky* was never realized, and the story "Amena" was printed as a fragment in 1846. Since all these stories appeared in journals of small circulation, they attracted virtually no attention. A number of poems and ballads which Tolstoy also wrote in this period were printed only in the 1850's. For it was only then that Tolstoy began to devote himself more seriously to literature, while simultaneously trying to free himself from his official duties at court. This process was difficult and took nearly a whole decade.

IV *Women in Tolstoy's Life*

Women so far had not played an important role in Tolstoy's life. But in the winter of 1850/51 Tolstoy met Sofya Andreevna Miller (née Bakhmeteva) "in the midst of a noisy ball." This meeting proved fateful. Sofya Andreevna was an unusual woman, with pronounced intellectual inclinations and artistic tastes. In many ways she was an antithesis to Tolstoy: being rational and logical where he was emotional, she prided herself on being a democrat and a Bohemian. She seems to have had a fine appreciation of music, an area of art which Tolstoy felt closed to him, and which gradually opened up to him under Sofya Andreevna's influence. Although not beautiful, she had definite powers of attraction; contemporaries mention her extremely melodious voice and her liveliness, and wit. Tragedy had overshadowed her early years: she had been involved in a romantic affair which ended in a duel and cost the life of her brother, Yury. When Tolstoy met her she was twenty-three years old, and had been married for four years to Lev Fedorovich Miller, a colonel in the Guards. The marriage had turned out unhappy, and the pair had separated. Nevertheless, for a number of years Lev Fedorovich refused to grant his wife a divorce. It was only in 1863 that Tolstoy could finally marry her.

A strong and self-willed woman, Sofya Andreevna seems to have resembled Tolstoy's mother with whom she vied for the poet's affection. Anna Alexeevna's refusal to accept her son's choice and her distrust of Sofya Andreevna may have been motivated not only by maternal jealousy, for she must have felt that in this relationship Sofya Andreevna would always have the upper hand over the weaker and more sensitive Tolstoy. Indeed, it was he who bared his soul before her, confided all his doubts, fears, and hopes, and looked to her for advice and help. Tolstoy's letters to his wife written over a period of twenty-four years show the poet's unwavering love and devotion and the influence which Sofya Andreevna had on his work; she was his prime critic, and her opinion often decided the fate of a work. After the poet's death, Sofya Andreevna kept up a lively correspondence with many poets and writers, among them Fet, Polonsky, Leskov, Dostoevsky, and Vladimir Solovyov. Some of them even sent their works to her and asked for her criticism. Fet wrote to her: "Already at Krasny Rog when I saw the books on your table . . . I was highly amazed by your intellectual capacities . . . There are many women who read; there are very few women who read poets and philosophers in the original; but I know of no other woman but you who reads and really understands [them]."[24]

Early in 1851 Tolstoy and his cousins, the Zhemchuzhnikovs, had staged a comedy, *Fantasy* (*Fantaziia*), at the Alexandrovsky Theater, which was even attended by Emperor Nicholas I. However, the lightness and frivolity of the piece annoyed the Emperor, who left the performance and ordered its removal from the repertoire. Nevertheless, soon afterward, Tolstoy was appointed Master of Ceremonies at the Court, and became even more closely attached to the intimate circle of the Imperial family. This did not produce any feeling of pleasure in Tolstoy, since his desire to devote himself to literature was growing steadily. "*I was born an artist,*" he wrote to Sofya Andreevna, "but all the circumstances and all my life until now have been against it. . . . I could never be a minister, or the chief of a department, or a governor . . . My real vocation is *to be a writer.* . . . I feel that I could do something good [in this area]."[25] His only satisfaction came from the few instances when he could use his influence at court to do some good. The arrest and exile of Ivan Turgenev for his article on Gogol greatly upset Tolstoy, although he knew Turgenev only slightly at that time, and it was primarily due to Tolstoy's intercession that Turgenev's case was reviewed and he was pardoned.

V *Beginning of Literary Career*

Tolstoy's real literary career may be said to have begun in the spring of 1854 when the journal *The Contemporary* (*Sovremennik*) printed six of his lyric poems, as well as humorous poems by "Kozma Prutkov" (the collective pseudonym of Tolstoy and his cousins, the Zhemchuzhnikovs). The poem "Bluebells" ("Kolo-

kol'chiki"), written in the style of folksong, became especially
popular among the reading public and made Tolstoy famous.
He was accepted into literary circles and became more closely
acquainted with professional writers—Turgenev, Nekrasov, Annenkov, Markevich, Pisemsky, Druzhinin, and others. However,
like his subsequently more famous cousin Leo,[26] Tolstoy never
became part of any literary group. One of the reasons for this was
his dislike of the "Natural school" (the precursor of Realism)
which had been proclaimed as *the* method in literature. "As
to the present 'Natural School' it is simply rubbish [*durnoy
khlam*], an inventory of furniture, and empty talk.... I cannot
be present at such readings without yawning," Tolstoy wrote to
Sofya Andreevna.[27] Of all contemporary writers only Boleslav
Markevich was close to him, and their relationship withstood
the test of time. Despite the obvious contrast between the poet-
aristocrat, and the "plebeian" writer of second-rate society novels,
Markevich became Tolstoy's close friend and adviser. Next to
Sofya Andreevna, Markevich was the literary critic whose judgment Tolstoy trusted most. Especially from the 1860's on, as Tolstoy's health gradually deteriorated, he came to rely more and
more on Markevich as his unofficial literary agent. Most of Tolstoy's theoretical views that have been preserved are contained
in his letters to Markevich, and although they disagreed on
politics, their mutual love of art bridged this difference. Markevich was present during Tolstoy's last days, and after his death
continued to propagate his work.

The outbreak of the Crimean War interrupted Tolstoy's literary activities. Although his high position at court precluded par-
ticipation in the war, he was anxious to take part in the events.
At first he tried to organize a guerilla battalion to fight the
expected landing of the British Army on the Baltic shores. When
this attack did not materialize, Tolstoy made a request to join
the army, and in March, 1855 he was enlisted as major in the
Imperial Sharp-Shooters' regiment. When the regiment arrived
at Odessa at the end of the year, an epidemic of typhus cut
down half the men, and they never saw any fighting since peace
negotiations had already started. In March, 1856 Tolstoy, too,
contracted the disease, and for a while his condition was serious.
Czar Alexander II was deeply concerned over the illness of his

friend and instructed the local commander to send him daily telegrams about his condition. Upon hearing the news of Tolstoy's illness, Sofya Andreevna, disregarding the gossip of society, rushed to Odessa and helped nurse him back to health. By the time Tolstoy recovered, the war was over.

Tolstoy spent the spring and early summer of that year in the Crimea in the company of Sofya Andreevna and his cousin, Vladimir Zhemchuzhnikov. This trip produced the cycle of "Crimean Sketches" which Tolstoy wrote soon afterward. Upon returning to the capital in the early fall of 1856, he found that his hopes for freedom had become even dimmer, for on the day of his coronation, Alexander II had named Tolstoy his aide-de-camp, and a few months later he appointed him as head of a secret committee to investigate religious sects. Although Alexander's choice of an honest and liberal man as Tolstoy did him honor, the poet was horrified at the task assigned to him. His letter to Sofya Andreevna shows him in deepest despair:

My friend . . . the day has come when I need you in order to be able to live. . . . The Emperor without consulting me . . . told me today that he has assigned to me tasks which are most unpleasant for me, and for which I am utterly unqualified . . . it concerns old-believers! No matter how much I protested and explained to him . . . that I am not an official but a poet—nothing helped.[28]

It was only in 1859 that the Czar finally accepted Tolstoy's resignation. "I realize," Tolstoy wrote to Alexander, "that everyone must be useful to his country, but there are various ways of being useful. . . . I shall always be a poor military man, a poor official, but I think that . . . I am a good writer."[29]

If Tolstoy's relations with the young monarch grew gradually cooler, he found an unexpected ally in the person of the Empress, Maria Alexandrovna. The former princess of Darmstadt was a woman of charm, fragile beauty, and strong mystic tendencies. Having married the heir-apparent at the age of sixteen, she had borne him seven children which had undermined her health and vitality. One of her ladies-in-waiting, Anna Tyutcheva, characterized her as "a soul . . . which belonged to the monastery . . . [a soul] that was pure, intense, constantly directed toward all that is divine and holy,"[30] while completely lacking in initiative and interest in worldly affairs. The Empress must have sensed a kindred spirit in the poet and drew him toward her small circle of *confidants*. Soon she became a steady and devoted listener to his works, most of which were read to her before publication either by the poet himself or by his friends. The novel, *Prince Serebryany,* and Tolstoy's only lifetime edition of lyric poetry were dedicated to her. Tolstoy's love and admiration for her lasted until the end of his life. "The Empress is an angel," Tolstoy wrote to Sofya Andreevna, "she understands me. She helps me."[31] It was probably the influence of the Empress and her support of his position that finally helped Tolstoy in obtaining his freedom.

Despite the difficulties which Tolstoy experienced in his career, he wrote a considerable amount of poetry. "I do not know why, but I have an irresistible desire to write—I start four to five pieces every day. The more I write the more I feel like writing," he told Sofya Andreevna.[32] During 1856 Tolstoy published over two dozen poems and ballads in various journals including *The Contemporary, Notes of the Fatherland (Otechestvennye Zapiski),* and *The Russian Messenger (Russkii Vestnik).* His success was especially great among the Slavophiles. Poet, critic, and Slavophile theoretician Konstantin Aksakov (1817-60), and Alexey Khomyakov (1840-60), poet, philosopher of history, theologian, and the most important theoretician of Slavophile ideology, were enthusiastic about Tolstoy's "folk" poems. They wanted to make him a poetic spokesman for their ideology. Although Tolstoy was receptive to some of their ideas for a while, he soon parted company with the Slavophiles, just as he did with the radicals (after 1857 Tolstoy ceased collaborating in Nekrasov's *Contemporary*), for Tolstoy found it impossible to align himself with any existing political camp and rejected all extremes, whether they be Slavophile, Westernizer, conservative, or radical.

VI *Tolstoy's Outlook on Life*

A man of considerable education and refinement, Tolstoy was cosmopolitan in the best sense of the word; he was equally at home in Russian and European cultures. Anything that smacked of fanaticism and ideological limitation was repulsive to him. Thus, although he shared with the Slavophiles a deep love of Russia, he could not agree with their interpretation of Russian history. "It seems to me," he wrote to Markevich, "that I am more *Russian* than all the Aksakovs and Hilferdings when I come to the conclusion that the Russians are *Europeans* and not Mongols."[33] He solemnly disavowed his earlier poem, "Our lord father, Peter Alexeevich," which had been interpreted as a criticism of Peter the Great's reforms—the crucial issue between the Slavophiles and Westernizers. "Peter the First . . . was more Russian [than the Slavophiles]," Tolstoy wrote in another letter, "because he was closer to the pre-Tartar period."[34] Tolstoy's bête noire was the Tartars and the Moscow period of Russian history which he regarded as a heritage of Oriental despotism that had fatally retarded the development of the country. Thus, in his work he tended to idealize the pre-Tartar period, while giving vent to indignation in his presentation of the Moscow period.

The narrow utilitarianism and materialism of the radicals was even less acceptable to Tolstoy, and as they gained power and importance in literary criticism, he fought back at them with the weapon of satire. Examples of this are his late ballads "Panteley, the Healer," "The Song of Potok, the Hero," "The Ballad with a Tendency," and the poem "Against the Current." What Tolstoy objected to particularly was the radicals' rejection of pure art and their demand that it must be didactic and "useful"; and so he exhorted his fellow artists to row "against the current" since "the infinite will triumph over the finite." Yet Tolstoy's polemics with the radicals were never bitter and vicious (in contrast to the latter's tactics). When Chernyshevsky, one of their leaders was arrested and imprisoned, Tolstoy tried to intercede on his behalf with the Emperor. "Russian literature is in mourning over the unjust sentencing of Chernyshevsky," Tolstoy is supposed to have said to Alexander[35] who, however, refused to change the sentence.

Although a monarchist, Tolstoy nevertheless saw the abuses inherent in the system, and was outspoken in his criticism. His ideal seems to have been a constitutional monarchy of the English type, and in Alexander II's early period his hopes for constitutional changes were not unfounded. But gradually, as the Czar grew more rigid and distant, Tolstoy came to realize his uselessness and eventually retired. "It is a curious fact," Tolstoy wrote in his autobiography, "that while the [radical] journals brand me a retrograde, the government considers me a revolutionary."

Despite his concern for contemporary issues, Tolstoy viewed them *sub specie aeternitatis,* and his interest gravitated toward things eternal rather than temporal. Love of art and beauty was inborn to him and had manifested itself already in his early years. The cult of art inherent in the philosophy of German Idealism was eagerly absorbed by him in his youth and remained an inalienable part of his philosophy. Tolstoy equated art with truth and devoted his life to its service. "I am one of two or three writers," he said in his autobiography, "who upholds the banner of 'l'art pour l'art' since I am convinced that the task of a poet is not to bring some immediate profit or utility to people, but to raise their moral level by instilling in them love for the beautiful which will find its application without any propaganda." Problems of art remained the most essential ingredients of his life, equalling the question of "to be or not to be."[36]

In a period of loudly proclaimed materialism and nihilism Tolstoy retained a basically religious—although not strictly Orthodox—view of the world, which owed as much to Schelling as to German mysticism.

It seems to me that the original state of our soul is a strong love of good or of God, which we lose after coming into contact with the cold substance in which our soul is locked. But the soul has not forgotten its first existence. . . . This is the reason for the feeling of the necessity of love which torments some people, and the feeling of happiness . . . which they have when . . . they return to their original, normal existence; if we were not fettered by substance we would immediately return to our normal state which is a continuous adoration of God.[37]

Throughout his life Tolstoy was interested in spiritualism, a subject in which he was well read, and he even attended séances by famous mediums. Thus, he was present at a séance by the famous Scottish medium D. D. Home (1883-86) who performed in St. Petersburg before the Emperor and the Empress. Two years later when visiting London, Tolstoy attended another spiritual séance by Home. In Paris during the same year Tolstoy arranged for a séance with the French magnetist Jules du Potet (1796-1881) and was greatly impressed by his powers. Toward the end of his life Tolstoy seems to have become fascinated with Schopenhauer's theory of reincarnation and nirvana, although he could not accept all of Schopenhauer's ideas. Tolstoy wrote to his wife:

I keep reading Schopenhauer and he makes a very strange impression upon me. . . . A bad one, because if you give in to it, then you feel complete contempt for others and for yourself; a good one, because all the unpleasant things in life seem so small that it is not worth thinking about them. But this again can lead to the desire to live without caring about anything, that is, to live dishonorably which, by the way, Schopenhauer himself does not allow—and there you have a contradiction again. I console myself with the thought that Schopenhauer is probably wrong, too, and that we cannot know the transcendental.[38]

All these views and his clearly expressed individualism brought Tolstoy into conflict with the prevailing literary, philosophical, and social trends. If a label needs to be applied to Tolstoy, he may be termed a late Romantic in an age of Realism, or a precursor of the neo-Romantic Symbolist revival of "pure poetry" in the 1890's.

VII   *Continuation of Literary Career*

The year 1857 brought the death of Tolstoy's mother. Although Tolstoy was sincerely grieved by his loss, it gave him a freedom of movement which he had lacked before, both in regard to his relation with Sofya Andreevna, and his desire to leave the court. For Anna Alexeevna had never become reconciled either to her son's choice of a wife or to a poetic vocation. The following year, 1858, saw the high point of Tolstoy's lyric production—over thirty poems were printed in various journals. At the same time Tolstoy's first narrative-in-verse, *The Sinner*, appeared in Aksakov's *Russian Colloquy (Russkaia beseda)*. This poem marked a transition in Tolstoy's work from the lyric genre to larger, dramatic works. Immediately after the completion of *The Sinner* Tolstoy began writing his second narrative-in-verse, *John Damascenus*, which was published in the same journal in 1859. Although the latter work is outstanding among Tolstoy's early poetry, it was hardly appreciated or noticed. Some critics felt that Tolstoy was too free in the treatment of a religious theme; others found fault with its form. Thus, Turgenev pointed to Tolstoy's "poor rhymes" in the poem. In a letter to Markevich the poet defended himself by stressing that his "poor rhymes" were part of a quite conscious artistic technique: "*Approximate* rhymes *within certain limits* . . . can be compared in my opinion to the bold strokes of the Venetian school which by its very inexactness or rather sloppiness, reaches an effect which Carlo Dolci can never reach . . . and which even

Raphael with all the purity of his drawing cannot hope for. . . .
I will not tire to repeat that I am not defending myself, but a
whole school."[39] And indeed, Tolstoy was only following a
general trend toward the "decanonization" of exact rhyme
which had been started by Lermontov, and which became the
accepted pattern for later poets.

Despite the fact that he was still Alexander's aide-de-camp,
Tolstoy obtained leave from his post at the beginning of 1860,
and went abroad with Sofya Andreevna. From Paris he wrote
to Markevich that he had completed the second part of a novel
which he had started in the 1840's, and which was entitled
Prince Serebryany. He further informed him that he had completed a dramatic poem, *Don Juan*. After a trip to England
where he saw Turgenev, Annenkov, Botkin, as well as Herzen
and Ogarev—the "official" opposition to the regime—Tolstoy pro-
ceeded to Dresden where he made the acquaintance of the poet-
ess, Karolina Pavlova. She became one of his admirers and
translators, and immediately started on a translation of *Don
Juan* into German, which met with Tolstoy's full approval.

VIII   *Retirement at Krasny Rog*

Tolstoy returned to Russia shortly before the emancipation of
the serfs in February, 1861, and retired to Krasny Rog, where he
personally read the Manifesto to his peasants. In a letter to
Markevich he humorously told of the effects of the decree:

It is unfortunate that the Manifesto is so long and unclear in that
part which is addressed to the peasants. I read it myself to them (in
addition to the priest) in three different villages. They, quite under-
standably, understood nothing, but seemed to believe my explanations
and conducted themselves quite well; there was no drinking, no refusal to work, etc. How great was my amazement when I found out
that in one of these three villages they removed the elder and the
foreman [*desiatnik*], and that they were about to remove my foresters
. . . and all this under the pretext that the priest and I had read to
them a *false manifesto*! Luckily, new explanations, with the Manifesto
in hand, and talks brought them to their senses . . .[40]

Known as a liberal landowner, Tolstoy built schools and hospi-
tals for his peasants and tried to help them individually as much
as he could. However, he was impractical and often chose poor
managers who enriched themselves while gradually ruining his
estates.

Staying in Krasny Rog, Tolstoy continued work on *Prince Serebryany*. The reading of *Don Juan* before the Empress had been
entrusted by him to Markevich who gave a detailed and encourag-
ing description of the reading. When Tolstoy saw the Emperor
a few months later he found him "coldly gracious."[41] Nevertheless, in September, 1861, he gave his approval to Tolstoy's request for resignation. Tolstoy's dream of liberty had been finally
realized.

IX *Tolstoy's Dramatic Period*

The 1860's constitute Tolstoy's "dramatic" period in contrast
to the "lyric" 1850's. During this time Tolstoy produced his most
outstanding work, the dramatic trilogy: *The Death of Ivan the
Terrible, Czar Fyodor,* and *Czar Boris.* A shift toward drama
had been already apparent in the dramatic poem *Don Juan* which
Tolstoy wrote in 1860. It appeared in the spring of 1862 in the
Russian Messenger, but received only little (and then mostly
unfavorable) notice from the critics. To justify his choice of
such an ethereal subject as Don Juan, Tolstoy wrote an open
letter to the editor of the *Russian Messenger.* Since the letter
in itself is an interesting commentary on the literary atmosphere of the time, it seems worthwhile to quote it at some length:

At the present time, when interests of vital importance are being
discussed in Russia, when so many social problems are posed and
solved, the attention of the public toward pure art has considerably
cooled off, and subjects which are outside civic life interest only a
few. Art has yielded its place to administrative polemics, and an artist
who does not want to be subjected to censure must dress himself in
the garb of a publicist, just like people who during the time of
political revolutions put on the cocarde of the winning party in order
to be able to walk safely in the streets. The opinion that art without
application to some civic aim is useless and even harmful, and that
it occupies a futile place in life has become widespread, and has
many supporters. . . . Not to admit in man an aesthetic feeling, to
consider this feeling a luxury, to wish to kill it, and to work only
for the material welfare of man means to take away his best part,
it means to lower him to the level of a happy animal, which is well
because it is not beaten and is amply fed. The aesthetic feeling in
a nation not only does not hinder its civic-mindedness, but serves
as its best ally. These two feelings must live side by side, and must
help one another. They can be compared to two columns of a temple,

or to two wheels on which the state chariot moves. The temple with one column is not stable; the chariot with one wheel limps on one side. But this is where the theory of the uselessness of pure art is leading to. This theory has been unfortunately quite effective recently. Indeed, our society is already quite unsympathetic to art. . . . In the face of such unfavorable circumstances a writer who devotes himself to "l'art pour l'art" must expect to get a cold or hostile reception from the majority of the public. Such was my position when I decided to appear before the public with the dramatic poem *Don Juan* printed in the April edition of the *Russian Messenger* . . .[42]

Despite this letter, the poem, one of Tolstoy's most profound works, remained unappreciated throughout his lifetime. In contrast, the publication of his novel, *Prince Serebryany*, in August, 1862, created quite a stir. Radical critics accused the poet of "aristocratism," "class prejudice," poor writing, and lack of interest in contemporary problems.[43] The general public, however, liked the novel, and this assured its success; in Tolstoy's lifetime three editions of the novel had been published, and it was translated into French, German, English, Polish, and Italian.

In the meantime, Tolstoy's health had begun to deteriorate; he suffered from respiratory difficulties and severe headaches. In the spring of 1863 he went to Schlangenbad and Karlsbad to find relief from his ailments. Every summer, from that time on, he spent at Karlsbad, but it seems that his illness was not properly diagnosed, and the "waters" gave only temporary relief.

Despite his poor state of health Tolstoy was extremely productive in the 1860's: In a letter to the poet Y. Polonsky in 1863 he mentioned that he was writing "a big tragedy in verse, *The Death of Ivan the Terrible*," of which two acts were already completed. A year later the tragedy was finished, and Tolstoy read it to his friend, the novelist I. Goncharov, while staying at Karlsbad. Goncharov was greatly impressed by the work, and put it on a par with Pushkin's *Boris Godunov*. A reading of the tragedy before the Empress at Schwalbach was equally successful. Tolstoy was greatly encouraged by such favorable reception of his first tragey. "[If it were to be staged] my reputation would be made—despite all the journals," he wrote to Sofya Andreevna.[44]

Returning to Russia, Tolstoy enthusiastically set to work on his second tragedy, *Czar Fyodor*, dividing his residence between his estates at Pustynka and Krasny Rog. Although busy writing, he was nevertheless interested in meeting other writers, exchang-

ing views with them, and furthering the cause of the "eternal and
beautiful." Tolstoy's literary connections in the 1860's were less
extensive than in the 1850's when he had resided in St. Petersburg, but they were now more permanent, and possibly more
satisfying. Ivan Goncharov was an interested critic and adviser
on Tolstoy's tragedies. Tolstoy made the acquaintance of the
poet, A. Fet—like him an adherent of "pure art"—who visited
him several times at Krasny Rog. Tolstoy corresponded with the
poet Y. Polonsky and the historian N. Kostomarov.

The poet's frequent sojourns abroad resulted also in connections with foreign writers and scholars, especially in Germany.
Thus Tolstoy was well acquainted with the historians, Max
Duncker and Ferdinand Gregorovius, the physiologist von
Helmholtz, and the botanist and philosopher Jakob Schleiden;
and he was on friendly terms with the philosophers Kuno Fischer
and Eduard von Hartmann. Schedo-Ferotti, Berthold Auer-
bach, and other writers kept in touch with him whenever he
visited Europe. Among them Tolstoy found intellectual stimula-
tion and views that corresponded with his own, but although
Tolstoy liked and admired Europe, he always longed for Russia
and kept in touch with all events there.

Work on *Czar Fyodor* progressed well, and in the spring of
1865 Tolstoy was planning to read it to Goncharov and to Kostomarov, who had been favorably impressed by Tolstoy's first
tragedy. The summer of 1865 found the poet again in Karlsbad,
where he underwent his usual treatments, while discussing his
dramatic work with friends. In the fall of that year he went to
London where he stayed for a few months and visited, among
others, Charles Dickens and Wilkie Collins. The search for a
milder climate led Tolstoy to Italy in the winter, and in Rome
he became a frequent guest in the *salon* of Princess Sayn-
Wittgenstein who became an ardent admirer of his talent, and
who introduced him to Franz Liszt.[45]

The Death of Ivan the Terrible, meanwhile, appeared in print
in January, 1866. Although the radical press gave the tragedy
a poor review, most other journals agreed on its merits. And
again, as in the case of *Prince Serebryany*, the reading public
assured the success of the piece. A motion was even made that
the play be granted the Uvarov prize by the Academy, and critics
like V. Botkin and Goncharov insisted that it must be staged.

Returning to Russia in the late fall, Tolstoy set to work on the
staging of his first tragedy. The strong backing of the play by
the Empress eliminated many difficulties; a large sum of money
was assigned for the production, and well-known scholars (e.g.,
the historian N. Kostomarov, the archeologist V. Prokhorov) and
artists (the painter V. Shvarts, the musician A. Serov and others)
gave their assistance. Finally, in January, 1867 the tragedy was
staged at the Mariinsky Theater in St. Petersburg in the presence
of the Czar and the aristocratic and intellectual elite. Received
with great enthusiasm, it ran before capacity audiences for
weeks. The public approval of the play by the Emperor silenced
those conservative critics who objected to some scenes in it.
"My defenders against the Chief of Police and those who are
'plus royalist que le roi' are the Emperor and Empress. They
came twice to see the play, applauded me twice, and called
me to their box," Tolstoy wrote in a letter.[46] However, the poet
was rather dissatisfied with the main actors, who did not know
their lines, and with the over-all slackness of the performance;
and it was only when the play was produced in Moscow in
1868 with the famous actor Nilsky in the title role that Tolstoy
was satisfied with his *Ivan the Terrible*.

The year 1867 was a busy one for Tolstoy. The staging of the
play had occupied a great amount of his time. He was still polishing *Czar Fyodor* and had issued a volume of his poetry. Karolina
Pavlova came to Russia with a German translation of *The Death
of Ivan the Terrible* which greatly pleased Tolstoy. While spending the summer in Karlsbad, he translated two ballads by Goethe,
and went to Weimar to supervise the proposed staging of *The
Death of Ivan the Terrible* there. The Grand Duke of Weimar,
Carl Alexander, with whom Tolstoy had played as a boy some
forty years earlier, was deeply impressed by the play which
he had seen in St. Petersburg, and had ordered its performance
at his court theater.

Part of the winter of 1867 Tolstoy spent in the capital. He had
made the acquaintance of M. Stasyulevich, the young editor of
the liberal *Messenger of Europe, (Vestnik Evropy)* and from
the following year on, most of Tolstoy's ballads and poems appeared in that journal. In January, 1868 Tolstoy went to Weimar
in order to supervise the final preparations of the staging of
The Death of Ivan the Terrible. The tragedy was produced on

January 30 and proved a great success. Its fate in Russia, however, was less fortuitous; after its run in the capital and in Moscow it was forbidden toward the end of 1868 in the provinces.

Tolstoy's relations with the conservative journal *The Russian
Messenger* and its editor, Katkov, had meanwhile deteriorated.
When *Czar Fyodor* was completed, Tolstoy gave it to Stasyulevich, and the tragedy appeared in the May, 1868 issue of his
journal. Literary critics again varied in their opinions from
complete condemnation to highest praise, but the chances for
staging a play in which the main character was a weak-minded
Czar were much slighter than those of the first tragedy. A special
commission charged with examining *Czar Fyodor* refused per-
mission for staging. Tolstoy was greatly upset over this, since
Czar Fyodor was one of his favorite works. He wrote to Marke-
vitch:

You know how I hate everything Red, but the devil take me ... if in
any of my tragedies I attempted to prove anything. In a work of
literature I despise any kind of tendentiousness ... I have said it
and repeated it, iterated and re-iterated it. But it is not my fault
if from a piece which I have written from love of art it becomes
evident that despotism is no good. So much the worse for despotism!
This [idea] would manifest itself everywhere, in any work of art ...
even in a symphony by Beethoven.[47]

Having completed *Czar Fyodor*, Tolstoy began work on the
third part of his dramatic trilogy, *Czar Boris,* of which he completed two acts by February, 1869. Simultaneously, having
become fascinated by the "Norman" period of Russian history
he began writing his "Norman-Russian" ballads. Traveling with
his wife to Odessa in February, Tolstoy was feted at a dinner
in his honor—one of the few instances of public recognition of
his literary work. The spring was very happy for Tolstoy; he
found nature at Krasny Rog especially beautiful and inspiring
and wrote a considerable number of ballads and humorous
poems. The summer was again spent in Karlsbad and Dresden,
where Karolina Pavlova met him "with a deep curtsey and
translation [of *Czar Fyodor*]."[48] Returning to Russia in the fall,
Tolstoy read *Czar Boris* to the Empress in Livadia, and was
encouraged by her preference of it to his other tragedies. He
spent the winter in Krasny Rog, polishing *Czar Boris,* writing
ballads, and trying to find a subject for a new drama. It was

only during the summer of 1870 in Dresden, that the idea for
a "human drama" set in medieval Novgorod took on more concrete shape. By the middle of September Tolstoy had completed two acts of the new tragedy, called *The Governor (Posadnik)*, which he read to Pavlova, but upon his return home,
finding that Sofya Andreevna did not like the play, he dropped
it, turning to ballads and poetry instead.

X   The Last Years

The last years of Tolstoy's life—the 1870's—again show a switch
of genre. The "dramatic" period is over, and Tolstoy returns to
the ballad, and to humorous poetry, as well as narratives-in-
verse. The works of this period, such as the serenely lyrical
ballad "Kanut," the gay "Match-Making," the famous satire
"The Dream of Popov" give no indication of the difficulties under
which Tolstoy labored. Financial difficulties were growing more
and more pronounced due to mismanagement and extravagant
spending, and Tolstoy was even thinking of applying for a
salaried position. His health was visibly worsening, keeping
him completely incapacitated over lengthy periods of time.
Having remained in Russia during the winter of 1870/71, he
traveled with his wife to Odessa in February. There he suffered
a severe attack of his respiratory illness which proved nearly
fatal. In his characteristic, humorous manner he wrote of it
to Markevich:

. . . Without exaggerating, I do not wish on the greatest scoundrel
among my acquaintances to be as sick as I was in Odessa, namely,
a cough and no strength to cough, and so you suffocate for at least
fifteen days. A doggish illness! I could breathe only while standing
on all fours, and in this position I sang, to the great dismay of those
present, "O Mathilda, idol of my life!" I am jocular by nature, but
I won't conceal from you—I thought that I could easily die (and the
doctors thought so too) . . .[49]

Once recovered, Tolstoy spent the summer again in Dresden,
reading Schopenhauer and continuing to write. "What a fool
I was not to have made his acquaintance when I could have,"
Tolstoy wrote to his wife.[50] In Berlin during the fall he started
on a "ballad without a tendency" which he called "Sadko," and
in Dresden that winter Tolstoy again picked up his tragedy,
The Governor, and began to rewrite it.

The spring of 1872, spent in Como, gave Tolstoy the idea for a narrative in verse, *The Dragon,* which was to be set in medieval Italy. Despite the beauty of his surroundings, however, Tolstoy felt unhappy and ill. The death of his wife's nephew, Andrey Bakhmetev, whom Tolstoy had loved like a son—the Tolstoys never had children of their own—was a heavy blow. His poor state of health prevented him from going to Russia for the funeral, and only during the summer did Tolstoy spend a few months at Krasny Rog, and then left again for Italy. Despite terrible attacks of suffocation and headaches, he wrote a narrative-in-verse, *The Portrait,* and the satire "The Dream of Popov." In December, 1873 the Russian Academy elected Tolstoy together with his cousin, Leo Tolstoy, members of the literary section. The winter, spent in Switzerland, Italy, and on the French Riviera did not bring much alleviation to the poet's illness, although the publication of *The Portrait* in the January issue of the *Messenger of Europe* (1874) and the congratulations of his friends gladdened him somewhat. In the intervals between his attacks he dictated poetry to his cousin, princess E. Lvova, hoping to bring out another volume of poems.

Treatment by a local physician at Krasny Rog during that year brought about an unexpected improvement. Tolstoy's pains disappeared and he felt reborn. Nevertheless, it was decided that he must spend the next winter abroad. With his wife's nephew, D. N. Tsertelev,[51] Tolstoy departed for Berlin in October, 1874, visiting Frauenstaedt, Schopenhauer's editor and popularizer, the philosopher von Hartmann, and many other acquaintances. In Paris, where they arrived in November, Tolstoy continued to lead a hectic and nervous life. The Empress who was spending the winter at San Remo on the Italian Riviera invited the poet to spend some time with her. Tolstoy felt well and accepted the invitation, amusing his royal patroness with tales and anecdotes, and reading to her his most recent poems. Joining Sofya Andreevna in Florence, Tolstoy wrote his last narrative-in-verse, *The Dragon.*

Tolstoy's final stay in Karlsbad in June and July of 1875 continued under the sign of apparent improvement of his health. "I feel unusually young, fresh and strong," he wrote to his wife.[52] With Turgenev, who was also staying there, he arranged for an evening of poetry readings for charitable purposes. Tolstoy

recited his early narrative-in-verse, *The Sinner*, and was grati-
fied by the success of the evening. Both he and Turgenev were
given laurel wreaths by their admirers. "I am bringing mine with
me," Tolstoy wrote to his wife.[53]

After returning to Krasny Rog, Tolstoy alternated between
attacks of his illness and apparent well-being. He himself seems
to have realized that death was near, but accepted this thought
with dignity and calm. The physicians attending him, however,
were apparently deluded and were planning another trip abroad
for him at the end of September. But Tolstoy did not leave
Krasny Rog any more. He died unexpectedly in his sleep on
September 28, 1875 and was buried there at the cemetery of the
small village church.

CHAPTER 2

Prose Works

TOLSTOY'S artistic prose is represented by seven stories of various lengths and the novel *Prince Serebryany*. In terms of volume, it occupies nearly one-third of his total production, the other two-thirds being equally divided between his poetry and drama. In terms of artistic significance, however, its weight is somewhat slighter. Tolstoy was a poet and dramatist rather than a prose writer, and his attempts in this medium belong to his earliest period when he was experimenting with different genres. Since Tolstoy dropped prose relatively early, he did not develop a distinct style of his own. Nevertheless, the stories and the novel are of definite interest in an over-all evaluation of Tolstoy's work, for despite formal variety, it is basically homogeneous. A number of motifs and major themes interested the poet, and he returned to them time and again. The supernatural motif in "The Vampire" and in the other fantastic tales is echoed in the early ballads, and even in such late works as the narratives-in-verse, *The Portrait* and *The Dragon*. The theme of Muscovite Russia and Ivan the Terrible which appears in *Prince Serebryany*, recurs in the "Moscow" ballads and is widened and enhanced in Tolstoy's first tragedy, *The Death of Ivan the Terrible*. In a sense, *Prince Serebryany* may be regarded as a preparatory study for Tolstoy's later tragedies. Thus Tolstoy's prose complements his work in his other genres and is at the same time a testimony to the poet's versatility and creative energy.

Tolstoy wrote his stories in the late 1830's and early 1840's. Which among them was the first is impossible to ascertain, but it seems probable that he started out with Romantic horror tales of which he wrote four: "The Vampire" ("Upyr'"), "Le rendez-vous dans trois cents ans," "La famille du Vourdalak," and "Amena." In addition, Tolstoy wrote two short hunting sketches— "The Wolf's Fosterchild" ("Volchii priemysh"), "Two Days in the Kirghiz Steppe" ("Dva dnia v kirgizskoi stepi"), and a humorous tale entitled, "Artemy Semyonovich Bervenkovsky."

I *"The Vampire"*

Of all of Tolstoy's tales, "The Vampire" is the longest, most complex, and ultimately most interesting. Even Belinsky who had no taste for the fantastic genre, found in it "the signs of a too young, but nevertheless remarkable talent with definite promise for the future."[1] And more than fifty years later Vladimir Solovyov praised the story for "the authenticity of its fantastic element." According to Solovyov, the fantastic element must never be completely bared, since this would demand faith on the part of the reader. Rather, it should only be hinted at, and there should always be a simple rational explanation for its manifestation. This requirement he finds completely fulfilled in "The Vampire," which presents "an amazingly complex, fantastic design on a canvas of commonplace reality."[2] Because of this skillful interweaving of reality and fantasy, as well as an admixture of humor, "The Vampire," despite its awe-inspiring title, is the least "horrible" of the fantastic tales. The plot of the story moves on two levels: on the realistic level it tells a rather conventional love story between Runevsky, a young man and Dasha, a beautiful orphan. On the supernatural level there is the story of an ancient crime and curse which runs through Dasha's family, and which involves primarily Sugrobina, her grandmother, a harmless-looking elderly lady. There is also an inserted first-person narrative about strange events in a haunted Italian villa which is told to the hero by a secondary character, Rybarenko, and which serves to reinforce the supernatural element.

Set in nineteenth-century Moscow, the story starts—rather curiously—with a discussion of vampires (upyri) at a society ball. The hero, Runevsky, notices a pale young man with prematurely gray hair (Rybarenko) and begins a conversation with him, in the course of which he learns that two persons present—an elderly lady (Sugrobina) and an old gentleman (Telyaev)—are actually vampires.

Rybarenko predicts that Dasha, the beautiful granddaughter of Sugrobina, whom Runevsky had already noticed, will die if she goes to visit her grandmother. Runevsky is greatly amazed at Rybarenko's words, but is inclined to believe him, since he seems to have valid proof for his assertions. However, when Runevsky is introduced to the alleged vampires and mentions Rybarenko, he is told that the latter has been known as insane for some time.

The supernatural level disappears while Runevsky courts Dasha in her aunt's house, where her wicked and ugly cousin, Sofya Karpovna, tries to spoil Dasha's chances. But it reappears as soon as Runevsky enters Sugrobina's house, where Dasha is visiting: an old book with a ballad full of morbid allusions and predictions falls into his hands.[3] The portrait of a young woman (that of Dasha's great-grandaunt, Praskovya Andreevna, whom Dasha greatly resembles and who died when her Italian fiancé, Don Pietro d'Urgina, disappeared before the wedding) becomes alive at night and speaks to him, but Runevsky is not sure whether this is dream or reality.

Returning to Moscow Runevsky accidentally meets the alleged madman Rybarenko again, who tells him of the strange visions which he and two of his friends had in a haunted Italian villa in Como, and which eventually cost the life of one of them. He also mentions that the villa where they had spent a night had belonged to a wicked old man, Don Pietro d'Urgina, who had once visited Russia, and who subsequently had been taken to hell by the devil in person. Runevsky begins to see some connections between his own visions in Sugrobina's house, and those of Rybarenko, and becomes fearful of the possible danger to Dasha. But he is unable to intervene, since he is challenged to a duel by Sofya Karpovna's brother for allegedly slighting his sister. Recuperating from his wound in Sugrobina's house, he has terrifying visions involving Sugrobina, Telyaev, and Dasha, but attributes them to fever. Only at the very end of the story, when Runevsky has recovered and married Dasha—after Sugrobina's sudden death—does the mystery surrounding the family become unraveled: it goes back to the murder of an old husband by an unfaithful wife, and the curse of madness and vampirism which the dying husband bestowed upon his heirs. It had affected Dasha's great-grandaunt, Praskovya Andreevna, who became mad and committed suicide after her fiancé deserted her. It had further made Dasha's grandmother a vampire who had already killed her own daughter (Dasha's mother), and was preparing to kill her granddaughter with the help of her associate vampire, Telyaev. The interference of Kleopatra Platonovna, an old governess in the Sugrobina household, who knew the secret, had saved Dasha, while Sugrobina was delivered into the hands of the devil. Rybarenko who turns out to be an illegitimate son of Sugrobina inherits a violent death: he flings himself down from a church tower. Runevsky is now completely "converted" and believes in the existence of the supernatural, but his wife Dasha and her cousin make light of the events and find simple and rational explanations for everything.

The grimness of the supernatural is lightened by occasional injection of humor. Thus, for example, not all visions in the haunted villa are terrifying. Antonio—one of Rybarenko's friends— has a vision or dream which is contained in a funny nonsensical vein: a golden gryphon "the size of a year-old calf" asks Antonio to come with him to Greece in order to settle a dispute between the three Graces. Greece turns out to be a big hall with a spring flowing from behind a painted screen in which beautiful nymphs are bathing. An abbé in a frock coat who plays the flute turns out to be the god Pan who wears clothes since "it would be indecent to go around naked" and who watches the bathing nymphs "in order to mortify his flesh." The mysterious death of Don Pietro d'Urgina who is carried off by the devil into Vesuvius in his dressing gown and nightcap also has humorous overtones. Even the vampires themselves are presented with some humor: Sugrobina's ramblings about the "good, old days" and about her late husband, the valiant brigadier-general Savely Ignatevich, are quite funny, and stand in striking contrast to her nocturnal bloodthirsty activities. Telyaev is memorable by his pet phrases about snuff, and his incoherent mutterings which seem to foreshadow Gogol's Akaky Akakevich.

As regards its theme and plot, "The Vampire" is hardly very original. The vampire theme, the heredity transmission of a curse, the motif of a portrait coming to life—all these elements were rather popular in Romantic literature in general. Tolstoy was well read in it and could have borrowed from a number of literary works.[4] One of the most likely sources, however, seems to be E. T. A. Hoffmann, who had been widely translated and read in Russia in the 1820's and 1830's. Perovsky and Vladimir Odoevsky had written under his influence, and it is certain that

Tolstoy was familiar with their stories, as well as with the German original.

Some secondary motifs in "The Vampire" are strongly suggestive of Hoffmann's tale "Ein Fragment aus dem Leben dreier Freunde": the story of Alexander's aunt, who is deserted by her fiancé just before the wedding, is very similar to the fate of Dasha's great-grandaunt, Praskovya Andreevna. The portrait of Alexander's aunt becomes alive and frightens her nephew just as Praskovya Andreeevna's portrait frightens Runevsky. Both "portraits" find peace only when their respective heirs are happily married. The story of Rybarenko's strange experience in the Italian villa may also have been suggested by the pattern of Hoffmann's tale where Alexander, Marzell, and Severin each tell their strange stories. The love plot of "The Vampire" on the other hand, bears some striking parallels to Perovsky's story "The Convent Girl" ("Monastyrka") which describes the tribulations of a young, beautiful orphan at the hands of her wicked relatives who try to separate her from her lover in an effort to induce him to marry one of their own ugly daughters.

There are certain weaknesses in the story, such as the paleness of the hero and heroine who are Romantic "types" rather than individuals, an overabundance of details, and the rather tenuous connection between the Italian and Russian protagonists of the story. Here, it seems, Tolstoy's Romantic exuberance got somewhat out of bounds. Still, despite these shortcomings, "The Vampire" makes for fascinating reading, and remains, in the words of Vladimir Solovyov, "a beautiful product of a vivid, youthfully fresh fantasy."[5]

II "Le rendez-vous dans trois cents ans"

Tolstoy's other fantastic tales are much shorter and less complex. "Le rendez-vous dans trois cents ans" consists of only some twenty pages. As its title indicates, it was written in French and remained unpublished in Tolstoy's lifetime. The setting is eighteenth-century France, and its heroine the young and spirited Duchess de Gramont. It is interesting to note that this is Tolstoy's only tale with a feminine narrator. Yet, Tolstoy conveys quite convincingly the image of a young and capricious noblewoman and shows amazing insight into feminine psychology and behavior. Again, it is a story about love and the supernatural;

however, the heroine does not directly participate in the fantastic events, but is only an accidental witness to them.

"Le rendez-vous" starts as a frame story, with the grandchildren of the Duchess gathered around her on a beautiful summer evening in her garden. The Duchess promises to tell them a story about ghosts in order to give them "chills" when they go to bed. She starts with a nostalgic remark about the past when everything was better—even the fruit. And, as if by chance, she recalls a basket of peaches sent to her by an admirer, the Marquis d'Urfé, who plays an important part in the tale. This light, conversational tone is characteristic of the whole narrative.

The Marquis d'Urfé starts a dalliance with the Duchess, at that time a young and beautiful widow whom King Louis XV had called "the rose of the Ardennes"—"a name which I well merited," she recalls. The motif of the portrait is again mentioned: the Duchess bears striking similarity to the portrait of her great-grandmother who had magic powers, and who scorned a presumptuous, wicked cavalier by the name of Bertrand d'Haubertbois. D'Urfé has a bad reputation in regard to women, and the Duchess's guardian, the commander de Belièvre, warns her of him. However, his remarks are of no avail, since the Duchess enjoys the attentions of the Marquis and delights in flirting with him.

Soon after, de Belièvre receives a letter from the Duchess's father in which the latter asks him to accompany his daughter home to the Ardennes, since he is eager to see her. The Duchess is vexed about the request since she suspects that the commander is responsible for it, and tells d'Urfé about her departure. He promises to see her in the Ardennes, since he, too, has an estate there. The Duchess is bored by the trip and torments her protector with comical complaints and feigned illnesses, all of which he suffers with the greatest patience and amiability. D'Urfé appears once and tries to kidnap the Duchess, but the vigilance of the Commander prevents him from carrying out his plan. The travelers finally reach the forest of Haubertbois which has the reputation of being haunted. Here, strange events begin to unfold themselves; a thunderstorm begins to rage, the horses are frightened, and the Duchess is thrown out of her carriage. When she recovers her senses, she finds herself alone near a lighted castle. She is greeted by a knight-in-armor whom she believes to be d'Urfé in disguise and whom she therefore follows without fear. Inside the castle she finds a large gathering of people in medieval dress and thinks that she has come to a costume ball. The knight expresses his love for the Duchess and his desire to be married to her at once. But when he lifts his vizor, she sees with horror that he is not d'Urfé and that the people around her are ghosts. Remembering her cross, the Duchess exorcises the ghosts, and they disappear in the air. The mystery of this strange experience is lifted at the end. Recovering from shock in her father's house, the Duchess hears the story of the wicked Bertrand d'Haubertbois who had committed many crimes and who had foresworn his soul to the devil.[6] Before dying he had promised to meet with his companions three hundred years hence—exactly at the moment when the Duchess happened to pass by. The story concludes with the Duchess's return to Paris where she soon marries another nobleman, while d'Urfé departs for Moldavia. The story concludes on a light note with the remark of the Duchess on the advantage of marriages of reason over love matches. The whole story with its abundance of witty, light dialogues illustrates well Tolstoy's ability to write in elegant and polished French. Furthermore, his characterizations of the lighthearted Duchess and the devoted, but dull, Commander are quite interesting and psychologically convincing.

III   "La Famille du Vourdalak"

"La famille du Vourdalak" forms, to some degree, a continuation of "Le rendez-vous." It, too, was written in French, and is told by the Marquis d'Urfé who recalls an episode from his youth while entertaining a group of aristocrats during the time of the Congress of Vienna of 1815. The vampire theme is developed against the wild, exotic setting of Serbia—possibly under the influence of stories by Merimée.[7] It is doubtlessly Tolstoy's most terrifying tale and sustains an atmosphere of horror from beginning to the very end.

Like "Le rendez-vous," "La famille du Vourdalak" is a frame story, started by an anonymous narrator who introduces the first setting, and continued by d'Urfé. Discouraged by the Duchess de Gramont, the Marquis goes away on a diplomatic mission to Moldavia. While stopping in a lonely village in the home of a Serbian peasant, d'Urfé finds his hosts in a state of agitation. He is told that the family is mourning the father who had gone into the mountains to fight the Turks. He left instructions to serve a mass for the dead if he should not return after ten days; but, should he return prior to that period, his sons should pierce him with an aspen stick, for he would be a vampire (*vourdalak*). The ten-day term is nearly over when old Gorsha returns from the mountains. His older son, Georgy, wants to kill him, but he is held back by his wife, his younger brother, and their sister Zdenka who cannot believe that their father is a vampire. The old man behaves strangely and refuses food and drink. During the night d'Urfé sees him creeping around the house and luring his grandchild outside. A few days later the child is dead. D'Urfé starts a flirtation with the beautiful Zdenka who reminds him of the Duchess de Gramont, but is soon forced to leave the family and to proceed on his way.

Passing through the same village half a year later, d'Urfé remembers his hosts and asks about them. He is told that the whole family perished through vampirism—each infecting the other. Zdenka has become insane from grief. D'Urfé is tempted to see the beautiful girl again and goes to her house. He finds her quite rational and even more beautiful than before. Carried away by her beauty, d'Urfé begins to make amorous advances to her, and only then does he realize that she, too, is a vampire. Shocked by this terrible discovery, d'Urfé thinks of flight. By a skillful maneuver he deceives her and all the other vampires of the family who had begun to gather, jumps on his horse and gallops away. The vampires pursue him and try to kill him, but d'Urfé manages to shake them off and escapes. It is, incidentally, a little cross given to him by the Duchess de Gramont which is instrumental in his deliverance. The tale concludes with a gallant remark made by the Marquis to his feminine listeners, in which he expresses his willingness to shed his blood for them— which he would not have, had he become a vampire!

IV *"Amena"*

The fragment "Amena" was to have been incorporated into a novel, *Stebelkovsky*, which Tolstoy never wrote. It is the weakest and least interesting of the fantastic tales, primarily because of

its stilted dialogues, poor characterization, and too obvious intent
at moralizing. It is possible that Tolstoy himself realized its
weaknesses and therefore did not try to complete it. Like the
earlier stories, "Amena" treats of love and the supernatural,
although the latter is not counterbalanced by any realistic explanation or humor. It is again a frame story, the setting of which,
however, is pagan Rome at the time of Emperor Maximianus.
An unknown narrator comes to the Colosseum with thoughts of
revenge over a rival in love. Suddenly a monk addresses him
and, telling him a story, orders him to desist from his criminal
intentions. It later turns out that the monk is the hero of the
narrative.

A young man, Ambrosius, and his friend, Victor, are Christians, sworn to eternal fidelity to each other and to their faith.
Ambrosius is, moreover, engaged to marry Victor's sister, the
beautiful and virtuous Leonia. When Emperor Maximianus
starts to persecute Christians, Ambrosius and Victor swear to
die rather than reunounce their faith. Soon, however, Ambrosius
is put to the test: he rescues a beautiful girl, Amena, from the
persecution of the Pretorian guard and quickly falls under her
spell. While Ambrosius is dallying with Amena (who lives on
the site of the ruins of a temple of Venus!), Victor is arrested
and thrown into prison. Ambrosius wants to help him, but Amena
advises him not to be rash and suggests that Leonia should ask
for mercy from the Emperor. When, instead of obtaining mercy,
Leonia, too, is thrown in prison, Ambrosius realizes Amena's
wickedness and decides to suffer with his friends. He is imprisoned, but is delivered in a mysterious way by Amena, who demands that he renounce his faith. Ambrosius succumbs to
Amena's charms and renounces Christianity and his friends. He
forgets everything for a while, but one day he hears that Victor
and Leonia are to be publicly executed at the Colosseum, and
goes there. He suddenly realizes his terrible guilt, exorcises
Amena whom he now understands to be an evil enchantress, and
publicly confesses his guilt, while Victor and Leonia are devoured by lions.

It has been suggested that "Amena" was written under the
influence of such works as Chateaubriand's *Les Martyrs* or A.
Maykov's dramatic poem, *Olynthus and Esther* which also
depict the conflict of Christianity and paganism.[8] However, in

the case of Tolstoy the religious conflict is not the main point, and is rather incidental to his general theme—the intrusion of the supernatural into everyday reality—which had loomed large in all his other stories as well.

V   *Two Realistic Sketches*

As mentioned above, Tolstoy did not attempt to publish all his fantastic stories. In contrast, his two "realistic" sketches were printed in the 1840's. However, since they are extremely short, they can be regarded only as preliminary studies in a different genre.

"The Wolf's Fosterchild" is a one-page narrative which tells of the author finding a dead she-wolf who had apparently nurtured a young fox along with her six wolf-cubs. The episode is presented as a curious case that could be of interest to scientists and hunters, and appeared in a journal for horse-breeders and hunters.

"Two Days in the Kirghiz Steppe" is a somewhat longer account of Tolstoy's hunt in the Orenburg area. Written in the first-person form, it describes the steppe, the various birds and animals that inhabit it, and records the conversations between the narrator and the cossacks who accompany him. Despite the fact that the language of the narrative is simple and bare, the author manages to convey the excitement of hunting and of life in the steppe. Printed five years before Turgenev began writing his famous "Sportsman's Sketches" this short story is an early example of lyrical "realist" prose. Tolstoy did not continue in this direction, and only during the last year of his life did he plan to start writing his "Hunter's Memoirs"—a collection of short stories and hunting episodes. Death prevented him from carrying out this plan.

VI   *"Artemy Semyonovich Bervenkovsky"*

"Artemy Semyonovich Bervenkovsky" is Tolstoy's funniest tale. It is written in the form of a travel anecdote which is somewhat suggestive of Chichikov's visits to various landowners in Gogol's *Dead Souls*. Getting stuck on the road, the narrator is forced to ask for the hospitality of the nearest landowner, Bervenkovsky, who turns out to be a crank. His two hobbies are: a very strict health routine and the construction of various machines with the purpose of building a *perpetuum mobile*. The first hobby becomes evident before the narrator has even a chance to meet Berven-kovsky. While waiting for the master of the house in the living room, the narrator notices a middle-aged man, "whose whole clothing consisted of a wig and shoes" running around in the garden. After running for a while, the gentleman stops and begins to shout in the most terrible voice while looking from time to time at his watch. When he finally meets the narrator he explains to him that he does this for his health, since loud shouting devel-ops the lungs, and invites his guest to participate in his exercises.

The second hobby, Bervenkovsky's construction of the most impractical machines is both funny and sad. For not only do his contraptions fail when he tries to demonstrate them, they are also ridiculous and wasteful. Bervenkovsky is wasting his energies and intellect while running after a chimera, and gradually ruin-ing his estate. The story of the old steward's attempts to keep his master from the "accursed petumebel" (*perpetuum mobile*) contains a note of tragedy. Bervenkovsky's farewell gift to the narrator—a coffee-grinder and an organ attached to the wheels of his carriage—break down as soon as the latter leaves his hos-pitable host.

These seven tales round out Tolstoy's experiments in the realm of both the fantastic Romantic, and the realistic short story. After having written them, Tolstoy abandoned this genre and turned to the novel.

VII *The Historical Novel* Prince Serebryany

Tolstoy's only novel is a late descendant of the Romantic his-torical novel which had been developed by Walter Scott, and popularized in Russia by various writers including Pushkin, Gogol, Marlinsky, Zagoskin, and Lazhechnikov in the late 1820's and 1830's. Tolstoy started on *Prince Serebryany* in the late 1840's; there are indications that the first version was in dramatic form. While spending some time in Kaluga in 1850, Tolstoy read parts of it to A. O. Smirnova and Gogol. But then a lengthy interrup-tion took place, during which Tolstoy wrote poetry exclusively. Only toward the end of the 1850's did Tolstoy resume work on the novel. He finished it in 1861, and it appeared in *The Russian Messenger* in 1862. In a letter to Markevich Tolstoy wrote: "I am

satisfied [with *Prince Serebryany*] . . . I wrote [it] with care and
love . . . as if there were no censorship at all."[9] Tolstoy's appre-
hensions concerned his characterization of Ivan the Terrible and
the whole Moscow period which, while historically correct, clearly
reflected Tolstoy's personal vision of it. However, no objections
by the censorship were raised, and the novel soon became extremely popular. It was reprinted three times in Tolstoy's lifetime, and was translated into French, German, English, Polish,
and Italian. There were also numerous reworkings of the novel
into plays and operas by various authors and composers.[10]

Prince Serebryany is a rather typical historical romance which
portrays both historical and fictional characters, has a fast-moving
plot with a multitude of breath-taking episodes, and a touching
love story. Yet, unlike many historical novels, history is not just a
decorative background in *Prince Serebryany*, but forms an inte-
gral part of the story in a moral and philosophical sense. Although
Tolstoy had intended to give an objective picture of the epoch,
he ended up by evaluating and judging it. In his preface the poet
confessed that while reading the historical sources "the book fell
from his [the author's] hands more than once, and he threw away
his pen in indignation . . . at the thought . . . that there could exist
a society which looked upon him [Ivan the Terrible] without
indignation. . . ." For his epigraph to the novel he chose lines
from Tacitus' *Annals* (Book XVI) which read: "Such slavish fore-
bearance and such a flood of blood shed in the fatherland weary
the spirit and fill it with grief; I ask of only one thing from the
reader: to permit me not to hate those who perished so inglor-
iously."

Two opposing ideologies are juxtaposed in the novel—the ideology of old, free Russia as exemplified in the fictional Prince Serebryany, and that of Oriental despotism and terror as exemplified
in the historical Ivan the Terrible. It may not be too farfetched
to assume that Tolstoy was not only idealizing the past through
his hero, but was also projecting some contemporary issues faced
by the liberal gentry—himself included—vis-à-vis the monarchy.[11]

The novel is set in the latter part of the reign of Ivan the Terrible (1533-84). It starts in 1565—the period when Ivan began
his fight with the old boyar families whom he suspected of opposition, and instituted the *oprichnina,* a kind of supreme police body
into which he recruited social upstarts who were completely loyal

to him, and who were used primarily to liquidate all the Czar's real and imaginary enemies. The novel ends in 1582, shortly before Ivan's death, when Cossack bands, under the leadership of Yermak, conquer Siberia and present it to the Czar. This historical framework provides the setting for the various adventures and tribulations that befall the hero of the novel, the young boyar Nikita Romanovich Serebryany.

After an absence of five years during which he fought in the Russian army against the Lithuanians, Serebryany returns to Russia. He is a man of upright, noble character, and completely loyal to the Czar. Yet without realizing it, he soon gets into conflict with the Czar's *oprichniki* who are terrorizing a peaceful village. Serebryany repulses the attackers since he considers them to be bandits, frees their prisoners (one of whom turns out to be a "noble" robber), and whips their leader, who swears vengeance. He then proceeds to Moscow where he goes to the house of an old friend, the boyar Morozov. It is only then that he hears of the many changes that have taken place in the country and in the Czar's character since his departure. Morozov tells him of Ivan's dramatic abdication, his institution of the *oprichnina*, the persecution of old boyars, mass terror, and mass executions. Serebryany is deeply grieved over Morozov's words; yet he does not criticize Ivan and his actions, and they both drink a toast to the Czar with the wish that God may enlighten him and soften his heart.

The confrontation between Serebryany and the Czar takes place soon after. Serebryany departs for the *Alexandrova sloboda* (the Czar's residence) in order to report to him on his Lithuanian mission. At a splendid feast he experiences the extreme mutability of Ivan's moods: after a graceful reception and praise, Serebryany is swiftly found guilty and condemned to death when the whipped *oprichnik* accuses him before the Czar. Boris Godunov, one of the "new" men in the Czar's entourage who understands his psychology and knows his fickleness, saves Serebryany. But Serebryany leaves the *Alexandrova sloboda* only to get into trouble again: when Vyazemsky, one of the Czar's favorites comes to Moscow to abduct Morozov's young wife, Elena—with the Czar's tacit approval—Serebryany defends his host and is put into prison by the *oprichniki*. Execution awaits him again, when he is delivered by his friends, the noble robbers whom he had aided previously.

Against his will, Serebryany becomes an outlaw; however, he manages to direct the forces of the rebellious robbers against an external enemy—the Tatars who had just started an incursion into Russia—and achieves an important victory. Despite the fact that he is in the Czar's disgrace, Serebryany returns to him to accept his judgment—both for his earlier escape, and for his victory. Ivan who had just personally indulged his bloodthirsty instincts in a mass execution in Moscow, is in a benign mood and offers Serebryany great honors at his court. But Serebryany refuses them and asks only for one favor: to be permitted to go to Siberia to fight against the wild tribes that inhabit the country. He goes and soon perishes there.

The love story which is interwoven into the novel presents a triangle, or possibly even a quadrangle. The heroine, Elena, who loves Serebryany, had promised to wait for his return from Lithuania. But in the meantime, she had been noticed by the Czar's favorite, Vyazemsky, a man of wild and uncontrollable temperament. To escape his persecutions, Elena accepts the proposal of the old boyar Morozov whom she had known since her childhood, but she does not tell him of her love for Serebryany, and this leads to tragedy. Serebryany's return clearly shows that Elena does not love her old husband, while the advances of Vyazemsky are not stopped by her marriage. Vyazemsky abducts Elena by force, but being wounded, he becomes unconscious and loses her on the road. Elena flees and finally takes refuge in a monastery. Yet, involuntarily she becomes the cause of the destruction of all the men around her. Morozov who seeks the Czar's justice is humiliated by him and finally executed.

One of the most dramatic and ideologically significant moments in the novel is Morozov's bold speech before the Czar when the latter "promotes" him to the rank of his official fool and forcibly dresses him in a jester's costume. Morozov's words serve to underline, once again, Tolstoy's own view of Ivan's reign:

. . . Czar . . . your new fool is before you. Listen to his last jest! While you are alive, the lips of the Russian people are sealed with fear; but your brutish reign will come to an end, and only the memory of your acts will remain on this earth, and your name will pass from generation to generation to eternal damnation, until the day of the Last Judgment! And then all the hundreds and thousands of those whom you have slain, the throngs of men and women, children and old men, all whom you have ruined and tortured, they will all stand before God, accusing you, their tormentor! And on that terrible day I, too, will stand before the eternal Judge in that very [fool's] dress, and will demand back my honor which you took from me on earth! And there will be no body-guard with you to shut the mouths of the accusers, and the Judge will hear them, and you will be cast into eternal fire prepared for the devil and his fallen angels!

Morozov's rival, Vyazemsky, perishes too. He loses the Czar's favor through the intrigue of another courtier, is accused of witch-craft, and is publicly executed. Since Elena considers herself guilty of her husband's death, she refuses Serebryany and takes the veil. The latter, as already mentioned, dies on the battlefield in Siberia.

Despite the fact that *Prince Serebryany* appeared at the high point of the Realist novel, in characterization, literary associations, and motifs it is Romantic. This is most obvious in the presentation of its main character, a variation of the Romantic hero—brave, honorable, naïve, and ultimately uninteresting. It seems that Tolstoy himself realized some of his deficiencies, for in a letter to his wife he wrote:

[I must] add some character to Serebryany, since he does not have any, and seems to be paler than any "jeune-premier"... I often thought about the character which I ought to give him—I thought of making him foolish and brave, to give him a good foolishness, but then he would be too much like Mitka [one of the robbers]. Wouldn't it be possible to make him very naïve, that is, to make him a very noble man who does not understand evil... who does not see beyond his nose and sees only one thing at a time, and never the relation between two things. If I could do this artistically, I could interest the reader in such a character.[12]

Despite his efforts Tolstoy did not succeed with Serebryany who seems to have the combined features of a Don Quixote and a Russian fool-in-Christ (*yurodivy*). All his actions vis-à-vis the Czar have an overtone of Quixotic foolishness as, for example, when he refuses to flee from prison, because he gave the Czar his word of honor that he would not; consequently, his friends carry him out by force. Serebryany's noble otherworldliness is underlined by Vasily, the fool-in-Christ, who greets him in Moscow with the words: "You are my brother! I immediately recognized you. You are just as blessed as I am ... we both are fools."

There is doubtless similarity between Serebryany and Yury Miloslavsky, the hero of Mikhail Zagoskin's novel of the same title. Published in 1829, *Yury Miloslavsky* was one of the first Russian historical romances which exerted a tremendous influence on writers and readers for many generations. Set in the "Times of Trouble" (*smuta*) at the beginning of the seventeenth century, it tells the story of Yury Miloslavsky, a young Russian nobleman who is torn between sworn loyalty to King Vladislav (the Polish pretender to the Russian throne) and his patriotic feelings; he is furthermore involved in a complicated love situation which seems hopeless, since his beloved is the daughter of a man belonging to the hostile (Polish) party. However, after many dangerous episodes all ends well: Yury is absolved of his oath to the Poles and regains his beloved. Not only are the respective heroes of Zagoskin and Tolstoy similar in terms of their basic "ideal" characterization, there is considerable parallelism in plot development, the presentation and function of secondary characters (e.g., the Cossack Kirsha, the magician Kudimych, the fool Mitya, in *Yury Miloslavsky* correspond to the robber Persten, the miller, and the fool Vasya in *Prince Serebryany*), and even in some individual scenes (e.g., Anastasya in her room surrounded by servant girls, one of whom sings a sad song for her, and a similar presentation of Elena when she first appears in the novel).

The supernatural motif which is rather typical for Tolstoy's early Romantic work in general, also crops up in *Prince Serebryany*. It is connected with the figure of the miller who has magic powers and whose fate is inexorably connected with that of Vyazemsky. Vyazemsky comes to him to get a love potion in order to win Elena and to find out about his future. The miller foresees Vyazemsky's and his own horrible deaths, but he cannot avert the disaster that awaits them, and they both perish in the Moscow executions. Another manifestation of the supernatural—Ivan's nocturnal visions of his martyred victims—has moral connotations and is symbolic of the torment in Ivan's soul.

Very much in the Romantic tradition also is the spirit of patriotism which pervades the novel and which unites nearly all characters in it, including the terrible Czar as the ruler of the land. Despite dissatisfaction with the existing situation, all major characters remain loyal to Ivan. Neither Serebryany nor Morozov contemplate desertion or rebellion. Maxim Malyuta-Skuratov, the son of Ivan's executioner who flees to a monastery, confesses that he may be guilty of "dislike [*neliubov'*] of the Czar, but not of treason," and that he would sooner let himself be beheaded than plot against his country. Elena in her final meeting with Sere- bryany exhorts him to go where the Czar sends him and to fight the enemies of the Russian land. The robbers, who lead guerrilla warfare against the *oprichniki* are easily induced to fight the Tartars and drink a toast to the Russian land, the Orthodox faith, and the great Czar Ivan Vasilevich of all Russia. The book ends on a strong patriotic note when Ivan is presented with the newly conquered Siberian lands.

With *Prince Serebryany* Tolstoy embarked on study of Russian history, a preoccupation which lasted the rest of his life. His main historical source for the novel was Karamzin's *History of the Russian State*. From it he took not only the basic facts of the reign of Ivan the Terrible, but also a number of incidents and descriptions. Serebryany's combat with a wild bear in the *Alex- androva sloboda,* the attack and burning of Morozov's house, the abduction of Elena, and other episodes are based on similar hap- penings described in the *History*. Tolstoy's descriptions of Ivan, Boris Godunov, and Morozov make use of Karamzin. The descrip- tion of the executions of Vyazemsky, Morozov, and others is based on Karamzin's narration of the Moscow executions of 1570. Ivan's life in the *Alexandrova sloboda* is presented as a direct quote from Karamzin. Nevertheless, as in his later tragedies, Tolstoy permitted himself some historical anachronisms in the novel, citing the example of Goethe who "cut off Egmont's head twenty years prematurely."[13] For example, the execution of Vyazemsky and Basmanov is placed five years earlier than it actually happened.

In addition to Karamzin, Tolstoy used a number of works on Russian ethnography and folklore, such as A. V. Tereshchenko, and I. P. Sakharov.[14] He tried to be thorough in his descriptions, and presented a colorful and picturesque cross-section of society, starting with the Czar and ending with the simple people and robbers. Tolstoy re-created sixteenth-century Moscow, he gave a detailed description of a boyar house, and showed a public duel and a public execution. Lengthy passages were devoted to de- scriptions of costumes: Elena in her rich dress of a married wom- an; Serebryany, Morozov, and Vyazemsky in their boyar dress;

Ivan in his regal costume, and so on. It was this picturesqueness which evoked the comment by Sollogub that the novel was "too lavish, [it] flashes too strongly like fire-works which do not permit you to rest for a moment."[15] Perhaps this quality was intended by Tolstoy to compensate in part for the lack of psychological characterization in the novel, for most of his fictional characters are flat and pale. The only possible exception to this is the historical figure of Ivan the Terrible. Despite the poet's obvious distaste for the Czar and all that he stood for, the image of Ivan is the most impressive one in the novel. Tolstoy followed Karamzin's interpretation of the Czar as a man of great moral and psychological dualism: highly intelligent and talented on one hand, he could be extremely cruel and bloodthirsty on the other. This psychological dualism is clearly evident in the novel, adding dimension and color to Ivan's portrait.

When the Czar is first seen in the novel, he appears in regal splendor at a feast where he is gracious and friendly toward his favorites, and capable of charming even those who know him well and detest his crimes. "Ivan combined with his fortuitous exterior an unusual gift of speech ... virtuous people listening to the Czar became convinced of the necessity of his measures, and believed, while he spoke, in the justice of his executions." Yet this same man is transformed into a fearful, trembling child in front of his old nurse during a thunderstorm which brings him visions of his martyred victims. Coldbloooded and treacherous in his dealings with the boyars and his favorites, Ivan does not stop even before condemning his own son to death. The full extent of his bloodthirsty fury is strikingly portrayed in the chapter devoted to the mass executions in Moscow in which the Czar himself takes part. Yet, this apparent monster prays earnestly at night for "peace in holy Russia," castigates himself, and is capable of clemency. And at the end of the novel, although aged and drawn, Ivan is still a wonderfully powerful and commanding figure when he receives the embassy from Siberia.

Compared to Serebryany and Ivan, the other characters in the novel are of marginal importance. Only Boris Godunov—a man of multiple facets, honest and deceitful, ambitious and selfless—is worthy of some note, mostly for his further development in the tragedies. Vyazemsky is a colorful and conventional villain, while Elena is a stock heroine—beautiful, pure, and lacking any individuality. It is a too obvious black-and-white characterization which is a definite weakness in the novel. The moral idealization of Serebryany and Elena who, despite passionate love for each other, strictly adhere to what is "right," taxes the credulity of the reader. Even more, the narrator at times intrudes into the story and further stresses the moral element. Thus, when Elena kisses Serebryany after their long separation, the narrator comes in with an ominous comment and warning:

The wily wife deceived her old husband! She forgot her oath given before God! How will she appear now before Druzhina Andreich [Morozov]? He will guess everything from her eyes! He is not a man to forgive her! Life is not dear to the boyar, his honor is dear to him! He will kill his wife and Nikita Romanych [Serebryany]; the old man will kill them!

Moral pathos is also partly reflected in the language of the novel which presents a curious mixture of solemn old Russian, imitation of poetic folk language which abounds in anaphoric constructions, comparisons, rhetorical questions and exclamations, and a simple, popular language. Solemn old Russian is used primarily in descriptive passages, while the poetic folk language is important in the lyric digressions of the narrator, which are strongly suggestive of Cogol's ornamental "poetic prose"; the simple language is used in the dialogues of the people (e.g:., Serebryany's servant, the robbers).

However, these three styles of language are not integrated, and possibly cannot be integrated at all, and thus create at times a curious, naïve effect.

Despite its shortcomings *Prince Serebryany* has remained popular for the sincerity of feeling, and its freshness and élan which were combined with quick-moving action. Sollogub who criticized the novel for its flashiness, noted Tolstoy's dramatic propensities, and recommended that he turn to that genre. And it was indeed to drama that Tolstoy turned within the next year.

CHAPTER 3

Lyric Poetry

TOLSTOY'S poetry is the most important and characteristic part of his artistic work. Tolstoy was a poet par excellence; he wrote verse from his early childhood until the end of his life. Extremely diversified in his formal means, he had nevertheless two dominant distinctive features: a strong lyricism which manifested itself in his lyric poetry, his folk songs, and the early narratives-in-verse, and a pronounced dramatic trend which is evident in his ballads, his late narratives-in-verse, and in *Don Juan*. His recurrent themes in poetry are the Ego of the poet (although Tolstoy is one of the least egocentric lyric poets), love, art, and Russian history. The supernatural motif of the early stories is carried over into poetry of both the early and late periods, showing clearly that Tolstoy never abandoned his essentially Romantic attitude. The tone of his poetry also remained basically the same and earned him the reputation of "the least tragic, the least disharmonious of Russian poets."[1] A "musical uniformity" based on an unchanging, harmonious Weltanschauung, a steady tone, and uniform linguistic devices distinguished Tolstoy's poetry from that of his contemporaries—poets like Fet, Tyutchev, Maykov, Polonsky, and Shcherbina—even though he shared with them an adherence to the "l'art pour l'art" principle. He never approached the bold experimentation with sound which characterizes some of Fet's poetry, the tragic dualism of Tyutchev, or the "imagism" of Maykov. Nevertheless, his poetry has a voice of its own, and an appeal and freshness that have not faded.

Tolstoy's lyric production is small: it amounts to only some 135 poems. Yet, despite its small volume, it is one of his most characteristic genres, and rightfully occupies a central place in the discussion of Tolstoy's work. The musical quality of Tolstoy's poetry is most poignantly expressed in these poems, many of which were put to music by outstanding Russian composers—Rubinstein,

58

Musorgsky, Cui, Rimsky-Korsakov, and Tchaikovsky. The latter especially found Tolstoy one of the most appealing poets, and his poetry "an inexhaustible source for musical texts."[2]

In his biography Tolstoy mentioned that he had started writing poetry at the age of six; however, none of these early experiments have been preserved. The earliest poem available is "I believe in pure love" ("Ja veriu v chistuiu liubov"), written at the age of fourteen. It is a youthful credo in "pure love" and "union of souls" until the grave, which is unremarkable except for the fact that it seems to set the tone for all of Tolstoy's subsequent love lyrics— tender, melancholy, and pure. The next poem, in terms of chronology, is "Farewell" ("Prosti"), written probably in the late 1830's. Here the motif of the "other world" which occurs in Tolstoy's later poetry is sounded for the first time: the poet consoles his beloved with the thought that even though they have to part now, they will meet in the other world where joy and happiness are awaiting them.

I *Lyrics of the 1840's*

It was in the 1840's that Tolstoy turned more seriously to poetry. About a dozen poems date from that period, although most of them were published only in the 1850's. Thematically, most of them are Romantic poems concerned with the poet's Ego, his feeling of loneliness, nostalgic reflections on lost youth, and on a happier, past age. Thus, the poet is seen traveling through a poor countryside, musing sadly about the pictures that present themselves to him—"Along the uneven, shaky dam" ("Po greble nerovnoi i triaskoi"). Standing on a rainy night at the window of an old mansion, he looks out into the darkness and thinks about its past glory—"A storm is raging outside" ("Shumit na dvore nepogoda"). In the midst of a romantically painted nocturnal landscape the poet recalls with sadness his earlier days: "The drops of an ending rain" ("Dozhdia otshumevshego kapli"). At his worst, he degenerates into sentimentality; at his best, he produces effective "elegiac" poems, such as "A Fir Forest" ("Bor sosnovyi"), the only poem which was published in the 1840's. It is a short poem which presents the poet in the midst of a dense fir forest, near a murmuring brook. The brook is mysteriously animated and asks the poet to return at night when it will tell him all that it has seen throughout the ages. Leaning on his rifle the poet listens to the waters while following his own sad thoughts. The tone of "graceful grief" is nowhere as perfectly expressed as in this poem which combines simple diction with pronounced melodious devices (syntactic parallelism, anaphoras, internal rhyme):

> I liubliu tot ruchei, ia liubliu tu stranu,
> Ia liubliu v tom lesu vspominat' starinu . . .
>
> I love that brook, I love that land (place),
> I love to think of the past in that forest . . .

In his general mood Tolstoy at this stage seems close to Zhukovsky, one of the first proponents of Romanticism in Russian poetry. There are also echoes of other poets in his poetry, especially the "Classics," Pushkin and Lermontov. Pushkin's famous poem "The Poet" (1827) is paraphrased by Tolstoy in a poem of the same title. And although Tolstoy's poem does not measure up to Pushkin's in poetic skill and expressiveness, the idea of the high and mysterious role of the poet which is common to both, remains one of Tolstoy's basic and unchangeable ideas. Lermontov's Romantic melancholy, his formal devices, at times even his diction, find reflection in Tolstoy, as in the "Gypsy Song" ("Tsyganskaia pesn'"), a tribute to the beauty and variety of gypsy singing.

Already in the early period Tolstoy turned to folk poetry. With a fine feeling for imagery and intonation, he succeeded extremely well in imitating the tenor of folk song. Sometimes Tolstoy combined lyricism with history—a feature which he later transferred to the ballad. Thus, in the poem "O, haystacks" ("Oi, stogí, stogí") there is an allegorical representation of various Slavic nations under the guise of haystacks. The stacks complain that they have been thrown far apart and that they cannot defend themselves against hostile ravens and jackdaws. The poem then goes over to an appeal to the eagle (Russia) to punish the insolent ravens and to protect them. In the original version of "Bluebells" ("Kolokol- 'chiki")—the poem which made Tolstoy's poetic reputation—there were also historical references: old, free Novgorod, Moscow and the boyars, and "all that has faded." "Bluebells" is Tolstoy's most famous folk song. Written in short four and three-foot trochaic lines, it consists of several rhetorical questions addressed to the bluebells by a rider galloping through the steppe. The first question: "My bluebells, you steppe flowers, why do you dark-blue [flowers] look at me?" ("Kolokol 'chiki moi, tsvetiki stepnye, chto gliadite na menia temno-golubye?") becomes a kind of leitmotif that is repeated, with some variations, throughout the poem. The first part is concerned with the personal fate of the anonymous rider; the second part presents a vision of Moscow and an embassy of Slavs from the West who are being kindly received by the Czar to the displeasure of the "Germans." It is probable that the nationalistic overtones of the poem, published at the height of the Crimean War, were in part responsible for its popularity. However, this element is incidental to Tolstoy's main theme in the poem: glorification of the past. The image of the popular, accessible Czar who steps out on the porch to greet his guests, the bold, carefree rider, create a *bylina* atmosphere and remove the poem from the present. It is ultimately less the content than its simple diction, songlike quality, and freshness which assured the survival of the poem until today.

II *The Productive 1850's; Philosophical Poetry*

The 1850's are the most important years in Tolstoy's lyric production: about 80 per cent of all his poems date from that time. Especially between 1856 and 1859 Tolstoy lived through a "lyric outburst" that was not to repeat itself again. During this time he wrote philosophical poems, personal reflective poetry, most of his love lyrics, the "Crimean sketches," and folk songs.

Tolstoy's philosophical poems are not numerous, and the term philosophical must be understood in a wide sense, to include the poet's thoughts on various eternal subjects such as art, the nature of the universe, life, death, and so on. Tolstoy was not a philosophical poet in the sense that Baratynsky and Tyutchev were. His philosophical poems are professions of faith rather than reason and are often incorporated into his love poetry, for love is the key to Tolstoy's universe. Nevertheless, these poems are important as a background for Tolstoy's poetic ideas which determine the tone of his poetry as a whole.

One of Tolstoy's most important themes was that of the artist and art, which he had already expressed in "The Poet." Another— and probably the most important—poetic statement on this subject is the poem "In vain do you artist, assume" ("Tshchetno, khu-dozhnik ty mnish'"), written in the early 1850's. It is an exposition of Plato's theory of ideal forms which had been handed down by the Neo-Platonists to the philosophers of German Idealism. Tolstoy stresses two points in his poem: the high position of art as a reflection of the "ideal forms"; and the unique position of the artist who is a creator and simultaneously only an imitator of the forms. Taking his examples from three spheres of art—sculpture, literature, and music—Tolstoy says that the ideal prototypes of their most representative works have "always floated above the earth, invisible to the eye," for "space is filled with invisible forms and inaudible sounds," but only he who knows how "to see and to hear" can convey them to others. The poem ends with an invocation to the poet to surround himself with darkness and silence, to be "lonely and blind like Homer" and "deaf like Beethoven" in order to create. Written in hexameter in heavy, rhetoric style with Church Slavonic diction, this poem is an early example of Tolstoy's "grand" style in poetry. Tolstoy's later poems on the theme of art, e.g., "He struck the strings" ("On vodil po strunam") or "Let him whose honor knows no reproach" ("Pust' tot, ch'ia chest' ne bez ukora") show him as a champion of pure art, his refusal to compromise and his rejection of the opinion of the crowd.

Tolstoy's vision of the universe—the second theme of his philosophical poetry—echoes the Romantics' and mystics' belief in a harmonious synthesis, and the role of love as the driving impulse in man's elevation toward God. These ideas are especially clearly reflected in such poems as "I, who in darkness and dust" ("Menia, vo mrake i pyli"), and "A tear trembles in your jealous eye" ("Sleza drozhit v tvoem revnivom vzore"). The first poem is a hymn to love, both in its earthly and divine aspects. The poet who had walked "in darkness and dust" has been elevated by the wings of love to unknown heights. A new vision of the universe becomes apparent to him. He sees it as one, organic whole, a manifestation of divine love which vibrates throughout nature. All things take their origin from it, are alive by it, and long to return to it. Although there are definite thematic and verbal parallels between this poem and Pushkin's famous "Prophet" ("Prorok"), the focal points of the two poems are very different. Pushkin emphasized the moment of revelation, and the final message given

to the poet: to "burn" the hearts of men with his words, echoing
the harsh grandeur of the Old Testament. In Tolstoy's poem,
revelation is only briefly mentioned, and the main stress is on
the vision of universal love which manifests itself to the poet, in
tune with the general tone of the New Testament.

The poem "A tear trembles in your jealous eye" is a combination
of a love and a philosophical poem. Starting and concluding with
an address to a beloved, the poet repeats the idea of love as the
unifying principle of the world: it manifests itself in the rustling
forest, murmuring spring, the beauty of flowers, and the look of
a fair maiden. Yet he stresses also the limitation of all these mani-
festations: they are only fragmentary reflections of divine love
which man cannot combine into one whole. Only when "earthly
sorrow" and "captivity" pass, will all be united in one love:

> V odnu liubov' my vse sol'emsia vskore,
> V odnu liubov', shirokuiu kak more,
> Chto ne vmestiat zemnye berega!

> Soon we all will be united in one love,
> Into one love, wide as the sea,
> Which earthly shores won't contain!

Interesting in its thought, the poem is likewise remarkable for
the expressiveness of its language.

The poem "A tear trembles" also indicates Tolstoy's preoccupation with the "other world," the third theme of his philosophical
poetry. Although Tolstoy echoes Lermontov in his Romantic
"*Sehnsucht*" for the other world, he reworks and tempers it with
pity for this world. Lermontov's youthful poem "The Angel"
("Angel") became the starting point for Tolstoy's poem "Along
the high heavens quietly, a soul flew" ("Gornimi tikho letela
dusha nebesami"). In Lermontov's poem a young soul descending
to earth in the arms of an angel never ceased longing for heaven:
the "dull songs" of earth could not make it forget its past blissful
existence. Tolstoy in his poem reversed the situation: the soul
flying through eternity toward heaven cannot forget the sorrows
which it has seen. And so it begs the Creator to permit it to return, so as "to comfort and to pity someone."

The motif of pity for the earth occurs also in the poem "In the
land of rays" ("V strane luchei"), which had the original subtitle

"From Swedenborg." The poet describes a "land of rays" invisible to the eyes of man where the souls of the dead glorify God in their prayers; all faces shine with bliss, for the grief of the earth is forgotten. And therefore, the poet begs his beloved to think of him in the hour of death, and "to grieve and remember" him in heaven until their reunion. Tolstoy saw the "other world" as a blissful existence when all would be united in a "chain of love" shining in the light of "eternal truth," oblivious of the past, devoid of individuality—a view which reflected in part the teachings of Emanuel Swedenborg,[3] in part that of Schelling. And so, death never became a poetic theme for Tolstoy, for it did not exist for him. There was one earthly life, and another, more sublime in the "land of rays." Thus, a high view of art, an organic vision of the universe which is governed by love, and belief in a more perfect existence after death make up Tolstoy's philosophical ideas as expressed in his poetry; and the tone of melancholy which is sounded in them becomes a constant leitmotif in Tolstoy's other poetry as well.

III *Reflective Poetry*

Tolstoy's "reflective" poetry is concerned with the poet's personal, rather than theoretical, feelings and thoughts. It is more numerous than his philosophical poetry, for Tolstoy is very much a poet of feeling. Here, as in his philosophical poetry, the term "harmonious" can be applied. Tolstoy avoids the extremes of despair and happiness alike; his voice remains uniform—sad and slightly resigned. The main theme of his reflective poems is the struggle within the poet himself and with life. The struggle within assumes at times a near-religious aspect, as evil becomes a reality—an "evil spirit" who tries to lead the poet astray: "There are days when the evil spirit troubles me" ("Byvaiut dni, kogda zloi dukh menia trevozhit"). Yet despite temptations and trials, the poet's belief in the voice of his conscience remains unshaken. Even though voices call him from all sides, he listens only to the voice which leads him along the "straight, holy road"—"As soon as I remain alone" ("Lish' tol'ko odin ia ostanus' s soboiu"). And in an enthusiastic tribute to the "holy convictions" of his youth, the poet sees himself on the old path where "truth shines as before": "I have recognized you, holy convictions" ("Ia vas uznal, sviatye ubezhden'ia").

If the poet's struggle within himself is thus ultimately successful, the fight with life is beyond his strength. This is repeated time
and again in Tolstoy's poems of the middle and late period. Life
is represented as a hostile, elemental force to which the poet feels
unequal. It has thrown the poet's "flaming heart" into the "cold
water" of society, where it burns in indignation: "The heart, burning more fiercely from year to year" ("Serdtse sil 'nei razgoraias'
ot godu do godu"). It is likened to a storm breaking the forest:
"There are many sounds in the depth of the heart" ("Est' mnogo
zvukov v serdtsa glubine"). Confrontation with life becomes even
an actual battle, as in "The Lord arming me for battle" ("Gospod',
menia gotovia k boiu")—one of Tolstoy's very impressive short
poems. Repeating the general rhythmic pattern of the earlier
poem "I, who in darkness and dust," it has two thematic parts.
In the first, God has armed the poet with "love and wrath" and
has shown him the right path; in the second comes an unexpected
turn—the poet has gone out to meet the "hostile storm" of life, but
since God had not made him "severe" and "inexorable" he has
been wounded and is perishing in an unequal fight.

IV   *Love Lyrics*

But the most important theme of Tolstoy's lyric poetry is that
of love. Tolstoy wrote about it from his early youth to his last
years, and most of the poems written during the period 1856-59
are love poems. Tolstoy's philosophical poems already gave an
indication of Tolstoy's treatment of love. As part of a divine feeling, love to Tolstoy is elevated and sublime. The erotic note, so
common in Pushkin and his contemporaries, is lacking in Tolstoy.
Yet, because love on earth is only a fragmentary reflection of
divine love, it is incomplete and imperfect. Because of this attitude, and because of Tolstoy's "balanced" temperament, his love
poetry lacks ecstatic, rapturous notes, but is rather uniformly
tender and sad.

Another characteristic which distinguished Tolstoy's love poetry
from that of other poets is its remarkable unity and cohesion. This
is not only the result of tone and form, but also of a chronological
connectedness, which creates the impression of a "lyric diary,"[4]
recording specific moments in the life of the poet. Also, as far as
it is known, all love lyrics are addressed to one woman—Sofya
Andreevna who became the poet's wife.

The most famous example from Tolstoy's "lyric diary" is the poem "In the midst of a noisy ball" ("Sred' shumnogo bala," 1851). It describes the first accidental meeting of the poet with his beloved in the midst of a ball, the impression she has made, and the feelings she has evoked in him. Many features characteristic of Tolstoy's love poems can be observed: use of sound images and comparisons instead of concrete images, parallelism of construction, and pronounced alliteration and assonance—all of which creates a strong, melodious effect. One stanza may suffice to convey the general tenor of the poem:

> Lish' ochi pechal'no gliadeli,
> A golos tak divno zvuchal,
> Kak zvon otdalennoi svireli,
> Kak moria igraiushchii val.

> Only the eyes looked sadly,
> And the voice sounded so wonderously,
> Like the sound of a distant reed-pipe,
> Like the playful wave of the sea . . .

Other poems complement each other in telling the story of the poet's love. Thus sitting alone in his room, he reminisces over the visit of his beloved, and cannot overcome his sadness and longing—"It is empty in my room" ("Pusto v pokoe moem"). Soon, doubts and fears begin to assail the poet. During a nocturnal ride, a double appears before him and derides his feelings: "Do you think that she really loves you, and that you love her?" he mockingly asks the poet. And using the expression from the poem "In the midst of a noisy ball" he predicts that the lovers will drift apart just as accidentally as they had met, "With a gun on my back" ("S ruzh'em za plechami"). In another poem, "The sea moves" ("Kolyshetsia more") the poet compares his feelings to the ebb and flow of the sea and expresses the fear that his beloved will not be happy with him for long. This phase of doubt, however, passes too, and the major part of Tolstoy's poems are devoted to reassurances to the beloved, consolation, and expressions of love. Thus, in the poem "Passion has passed" ("Minula strast'"), the poet reassures his beloved that his love for her has remained the same, even though "passion has passed." He feels his love especially keenly when he is far from her and hopes that she thinks of him, too, at the same hour, "Since the time that I am alone" ("S tekh por kak ia odin"). He tries to console her and asks her to lean on him for support and protection. He calls on her to forget the past and to look ahead.

In the center of Tolstoy's love poetry stands the image of his beloved. Incorporeal, sad, and mysterious as she appeared in the early poem "In the midst of a noisy ball," she remains the same in his later poetry. The inconcreteness of the beloved is expressed at times through elaborate imagery which tends to obscure the real image, or simply by the address "you," "friend." In all poems she is a nebulous vision with "sad eyes grieving as before." Grief and sadness become constant leitmotifs in her description and are repeated in every poem. There is not a single poem where she is not sad, bent, or suffering. Tears tremble in her eyes, her heart is aching, and she seems to be "fading away uselessly." If she could only see her own sadness, exclaims the poet, how she would weep over herself. "My sad friend," "my poor friend" he addresses her, stressing the sadness of her image. Viewing her grief, the poet's only hope is that sleep will pour forgetfulness over the wounds of her heart. Even in the "Crimean Sketches," Tolstoy's happiest poems, the beloved is seen "filled with her usual sorrow" or gazing sadly over an abyss in the midst of a beautiful evening landscape.

The poet never explains this grief, as if he wanted to leave the aura of mystery which surrounded his beloved in the earliest poems. In a few poems there is a hint that her sadness is akin to Tolstoy's own, a longing for the "heavenly home" which had been mentioned in his philosophical poems. Thus in the poem "Now the last snow is melting in the fields" ("Vot uzh sneg poslednii v pole taet") the poet presents the beauty of spring in glowing tones: the snow is beginning to thaw, the flowers open up, the cranes are calling to each other, "everything has been warmed by the breath of spring." Yet the beloved is seen sad as usual against this background of happiness. "Why is it so dark in your soul?" the poet asks her, and gives himself the answer to his question: she would like to fly to "the native land" without regrets for the "earthly spring." In the poem "Do not try to restrain your troubled spirit" ("O ne pytaisia dukh uniat' trevozhnyi") the poet recognizes the grief of the beloved and tries to console her by a promise of harmony in the "final hour."

Tolstoy's attitude in most poems remains also essentially the same—melancholy, tender, and slightly resigned. Most of the time he speaks to his beloved, tries to console her, and pleads with her to forget her grief. At the same time it seems as if he himself felt that he could not overcome her sadness or share in it. This half-heartedness is formally expressed by the frequent use of negative exhortations: "Oh, do not try to restrain your troubled spirit!" he exclaims in one poem. "Oh do not hasten where life is lighter and purer!" he begs her in another poem. "Do not regret what has been," he tells her.

Tolstoy's love lyrics oscillate between those of ornate, elaborate imagery and simple poems with a conversational tone. The best example of the first type is the poem "Into my soul filled with insignificant vanity" ("Mne v dushu, polnuiu nichtozhnoi suety"). Written at about the same time as the philosophical poem "I, who in darkness and dust," it is connected with it by the motif of the elevating power of love as well as by its solemn diction and complex imagery and syntax. The metaphorical garden of the poet's soul, filled with flowers of vanity, has been suddenly uprooted by the whirlwind of passion. Tears like a beneficial rain water the devastated soul of the poet, heralding a new, better life. The poem ends with an unresolved metaphor in which the poet is presented as standing over the ruins, listening to the distant thunder. Despite the banality of some of the imagery, Tolstoy achieves remarkable effects by his skillful use of diction and rhythm:

> I nad oblomkami bezmolven ia stoiu,
> I, trepetom eshche nevedomym ob'iatyi,
> Voskresnuvshego dnia p'iu svezhuiu struiu
> I groma dal'nego vnimaiu perekaty . . .

> And I stand, mute, above the ruins
> And filled with an unknown trepidation,
> I drink the air of the resurrected day
> And listen to the distant rumblings of thunder

In his later love poems, Tolstoy tends to be quite simple in imagery and language. Still, he achieves poems of rare beauty by this simplicity and an intimacy of tone. One such example is the poem "It was getting dark, the hot day was growing pale" ("Smerkalos', zharkii den' blednel neulovimo"). The charm of the poem lies in an impressionistic sketching of nature and of his

beloved, as well as harmony of mood. The poem starts with the
description of a quiet summer evening, with a mist floating above
the lake. The image of his beloved appears before the poet with
"sad eyes grieving as before." There is harmony between nature
and the beloved, a blending of the two images, and an atmosphere
of calm and peace. The language is extremely simple, with emotional epithets used in connection with the beloved who dominates the poem, as she does in most of Tolstoy's love lyrics.

Despite its relatively narrow range, Tolstoy's love poetry is
unique in its directness, warmth, and quiet dignity of feeling
which the poet conveys. The poet's more objective side manifests
itself in the "Crimean Sketches" and in his folk songs.

V *"The Crimean Sketches"*

The "Crimean Sketches" ("Krymskie ocherki") occupy a unique
position among Tolstoy's lyric poetry. They are the most objective
poems which Tolstoy wrote. Even though the figure of the poet is
in the background of many of them it is that of a detached—and
usually delighted—observer. And although the image of the beloved appears in some of the poems (Sofya Andreevna actually
accompanied the poet on the trip), she does not dominate them as
she did the love poems. The "Sketches" are Tolstoy's happiest
poems, and in a few of them the humorous note, which is lacking
in the other lyric poems, asserts itself.

The title for the cycle may have been suggested by Mickie-
wicz's "Crimean Sonnets" which, like the "Crimean Sketches,"
were the result of a journey and a love experience. However, apart
from the title there is hardly any similarity between the strictly
form-oriented, intensely personal, sometimes symbolical, and
solemn poetry of the Polish poet, and the formally diverse, detached, and gay poems of Tolstoy. Tolstoy's "Sketches" contain
fourteen poems, although not all of them were published simultaneously. Eleven poems appeared in 1856, while three others
were printed only in 1867. Originally, Tolstoy had included four
more poems in the cycle, but had deleted them later on.[5]

The poems are not connected; they simply record scenery, impressions, moods, juxtaposing reality and dream, past and present.
Thus, the poet describes a mountain ridge where winter winds
howl and contrasts it to a peaceful valley where the laurel is

blooming above an "eternally blue" sea, ("Over the inaccessible steepness"/"Nad nepristupnoi krutiznoi"). He recalls an expedition to Chatyr-Dag mountain when he and his companions were creeping "like flies" along the cliffs, and humorously praises the dexterity of man, ("By the almighty will of Allah"/"Vsesil'noi voleiu Allakha"). He captures the impression of a hot noon near a murmuring brook ("The hot noon invites to laziness"/"Klonit k leni polden' zhguchii"); he describes the changing colors of the sea before a storm ("The sun is hot"/"Solntse zhzhet"). A beautiful evening with a nightingale singing creates a mood of happiness ("Do you remember the evening, when the sea was murmuring"/"Ty pomnish' li vecher, kak more shumelo"); the description of a summer night in the mountains is followed by the poet's vision of himself and his beloved riding along an abyss; the line between dream and reality is obliterated, and the poet concludes with the wish not to awaken—if this is indeed a dream, ("The fog lifts"/"Tuman vstaet").

The recent Crimean War is mentioned, as in the poem where the poet wistfully complains of the "scorpios, centipeds, and Englishmen" who spoil the beauty of the landscape for him ("How wondrously beautiful you are"/"Kak chudesno khoroshi vy"), or when he describes a house partly destroyed by the enemy ("I greet you, devastated house"/"Privetstvuiu tebia, opustashennyi dom"). The past is evoked in such poems as "Hard is our path" ("Tiazhel nash put' ") or "Where the clear spring" ("Gde svetlyi kliuch' ") which are among the best poems of the cycle.

The first poem describes a deserted town high in the mountains. According to tradition it was built by the "sons of Israel" who fled from a foreign yoke to live in peace. But the wrath of God did not leave them, and the town has died out leaving only a few people who walk "like shadows" among he ruins. The use of Church Slavonic vocabulary and of a simple syntax give an air of biblical solemnity to the poem. The second poem may have been written under the influence of André Chénier whom Tolstoy was translating at the time, especially his poem "Bacchus." It presents a vision of ancient Greece which had once extended to the Crimea. A poetic past which consists of a mixture of reality and mythology is contrasted with a sad present: lions and centaurs, goats and satyrs used to play around the clear spring; Bacchantes celebrated their feasts to the sounds of "tympanums, flutes and lyre";

and the chariot of Diana used to pass along the sea at night. Now all this has disappeared; there are no traces of "happy Greece," and only a "taciturn Tatar" can be seen tending his flock. The final lines of the poem are among the most felicitous which Tolstoy had written:

> I vse proshlo; nigde sleda
> Ne vidno Gretsii schastlivoi,
> Bez tainy les, bez pliasok nivy,
> Bez pesnei pestrye stada
> Paset tatarin molchalivyi . . .

> And everything has passed; there is nowhere
> A trace of happy Greece,
> The forest has no mystery, the fields have no dances,
> Without songs, a taciturn Tatar
> Tends his multicolored flock . . .

If there are broad, general themes in the "Crimean Sketches" it is the beauty of the Crimean landscape and the feeling of happiness and joy of life which had communicated itself to the poet.

VI *Folk Poems*

Tolstoy's folk poems of the 1850's are not numerous, yet they are extraordinary in their closeness to actual folk songs. Tolstoy achieved this effect by borrowing, at times, words, expressions, or even lines from well-known songs. He used many distinctive features of folk song, such as symbolic parallelism, fixed epithets, and tonic, unrhymed verse.

In contrast to such early poems as "Bluebells," Tolstoy's later folk poems are concerned with such eternal themes as love, grief, and life itself. Love is very often connected with grief. Thus, in the poem "If only I knew" ("Kaby znala ia, kaby vedala") a young girl speaks about the grief which love has brought her: had she known that she would suffer, she would not have looked at the young man when he first came. Now she cannot stop thinking of him and lives in the hope of seeing him again. A more tragic note is sounded in the poem "Why, evil fate" ("Ty pochto, zlaia kruchinushka") where a married woman bemoans her fate of being torn between her former family and her husband. In the poem "O, you mother-grief" ("Uzh ty mat' toska"), written from the point of view of a man, love and grief become synonymous. A young man asks grief how it attacks man: Does it come as a snake, or as a vulture, or as a wolf, or as a knight with many servants? But grief merely says it comes in the shape of a young, beautiful girl, and the young man himself will voluntarily go and meet her.

To the theme of grief without love are devoted a number of poems, such as "O my corn field" (Uzh ty niva moia"), "A wreathe of white mist" ("Griadoi klubitsia beloiu"), and "You, unknown" ("Ty nevedomoe, neznamoe"). In some of them the poet uses complex parallelism to express his ideas. For example, in the poem "O my corn field," a comparison is made between the field and human thought. Like the wind which bends ears of corn and scatters its seed, so are scattered human thoughts, out of which grief grows. In the poem "A wreathe of white mist," a parallel is drawn between grief and mist: a mist rises above a lake, while a young man is weighed down by grief. However, the mist will disperse, while grief will remain with him forever. In the poem "You, unknown," based on a folk song and the seventeenth-century anonymous tale of "Woe-Misfortune" ("Gore-Zloschastie") grief is presented as an unknown, invisible force which defeats the hero of the poem. The poem starts with an address by the young man and is followed by his tale of how he is being tempted. Grief tells him not to hurry with his work; it rises as a tavern on his way; it buzzes around him like a fly. The final lines imply the defeat of the young man and his lapse into idleness.

The theme of fight with life is expressed in such poems as "No, friends, I won't know any sleep or peace" ("Net, uzh ne vedat' mne, bratsy, ni sna ni pokoiu") and "Long live you, life" ("Ispolat' tebe, zhizn"). In both poems life is presented as an old, clamoring woman that has attacked the hero. In the second poem, the fight of life is connected with the theme of song. The noise and clamor of the old woman—life—has deafened the sounds of the *gusli*, (a four-stringed instrument like the harp) and has trampled on the flowers which were growing through grief. The poem ends with a plea for freedom and song. Thus, except for their form, Tolstoy's folk poems seem to echo the themes of his reflective poetry and to reinforce some of the ideas expressed through it.

VII *Last Lyric Poems*

The 1860's were Tolsoy's dramatic period, during which he wrote only a few lyric poems, and it was only during the last five years of his life that he again turned to lyric poetry. There are about a dozen poems which he wrote during that period. For the most part, they are personal poems which express the poet's thoughts and feelings. There is a marked restraint in tone, greater objectivity, and a quiet dignity which sets these poems apart from earlier poetry. The poet's formal mastery had reached its peak; a more "prosaic" diction asserts itself, possibly under the influences of his late narratives-in-verse.

The theme of fight with life also comes up in such poems as "In a deserted monastery near Cordoba" ("V monastyre pustyn-nom bliz Kordovy"), and "I heard about the deed of the fighter of Crotona" ("Pro podvig slyshal ja Krotonskogo boitsa"). The first part of the first poem describes a painting which shows a saint being skinned alive; the second part introduces an unexpected parallel: the poet feels kinship with the saint, for from his soul, too, all covers have been torn off, and every touch of life is "torment" and "agony." In the second poem Tolstoy uses the legend about Milo of Crotona who allegedly carried a heifer around his neck in order to increase his physical strength. Like Milo, the poet put grief on his shoulders in his youth, not realizing the heaviness of the burden. Now he has turned gray, but grief continues growing, sapping his strength. But most poems are objective, calm pictures of nature and of the poet's mood.

Spring is evoked in the poem "The door has opened up again" ("Vnov' rastvorilas' dver' "). An interesting description of a hunt, which approaches prose in its diction, is presented in the poem "At the hunt" ("Na tiage"); only at the very end of the poem, does Tolstoy introduce a personal note by remembering his "former joys" and "forgotten sorrows." A picture of golden autumn evokes in the poet the thought about his artistic harvest, and he asks himself whether he has been successful in the service of beauty: "The transparent clouds" ("Prozrachnykh oblakov").[6]

One of Tolstoy's most famous love lyrics "It was in early spring" ("To bylo ranneiu vesnoi")—a kind of "pendant" to the early poem "In the midst of a noisy ball"—evokes with melancholy the early days of spring, youth, and love. In this poem Tolstoy returns to his earlier, more melodious formal devices, and the phrase "It was in early spring" becomes a leitmotif throughout. Tolstoy's last poem, "The earth was in bloom" ("Zemlia tsvela"), was apparently completed shortly before his death. In content and form (it was written in octaves) it displays his usual mastery. He again describes his favorite season, spring; however, this time it becomes the starting point for the portrayal of a strange, mystic experience: the poet suddenly feels union with nature, and at the same time he experiences peace of mind and loss of desire. He realizes that this is the ideal state for creativity and concludes with the exhortation to "captivate the moment," for the interval between dream and wakefulness is short. This poem seems to reflect Tolstoy's preoccupation with Schopenhauer.

VIII   Tolstoy's "Impressionism"

Tolstoy is considered to be one of the initiators of "Impressionist" lyric poetry—that is poetry which tends to create a specific poetic mood, an impression of an experience rather than a concrete rendering of it. An analysis of Tolstoy's poems shows that this "Impressionism" is the result of various devices: the subordination of concrete images to the general mood of the poem; general, vague, and colorless descriptions; an accumulation of images which ultimately cancel each other; stress on imagery of sound rather than imagery of vision.

This tendency can already be seen in the earliest poems, where descriptions of nature are usually subordinated to the expression of the poet's melancholy feelings. Thus, in "A fir forest" only the two initial lines describe the setting, while the rest of the poem is devoted to the tale of the brook and the feelings evoked by it in the poet. In Tolstoy's love poetry the emphasis on feeling is, obviously, especially strong. Description plays a very small part in it, while emotional epithets determine its characters. Among the most frequent epithets used are "sad," "restless,' "heavy," "tormenting," "dear," "poor," and "tender."

In Tolstoy's later poetry, descriptions become the starting point for a representation of the poet's feelings or moods. Yet, despite their importance, these descriptions are often brief, sketchy, and devoid of color. In the poem "It was getting dark" ("Smerkalos'. Zharkii den' blednel nuelovimo") the poet describes an evening near a lake: it is an impressionistic sketch of twilight, of a day "growing pale," and of a "cloud of fog" against which his beloved floats with sad eyes, "grieving as before."

In poems where Tolstoy is more descriptive, the color scheme is pale, while the imagery tends to repeat itself. In the poem "Now the last snow is thawing in the field" ("Vot uzh sneg poslednii v pole taet"), which has one of Tolstoy's most concrete descriptions of spring, he mentions only the blue of the flowers and the green of the forest. Only in a few poems is there brightness of description, such as one poem of the "Crimean Sketches," in which he describes a landscape with a brook flowing over gray stones, while red roses climb on black cypress trees ("Where the clear spring").

One of the most interesting impressionisic methods used by Tolstoy is his accumulation of images. This "stringing" (*nanizyvanie*) of images is best seen in such poems as "You are a victim of life's troubles" ("Ty zhertva zhiznenykh trevog") or "It is not the wind blowing from high" ("Ne veter, veia s vysoty"). In the first poem, the poet conveys the image of his melancholy beloved through a series of disconnected nature images. In the first stanza she is compared to a torn leaf carried by the wind; in the second stanza she is likened to gray smoke driven by the wind; in the third stanza she is compared to apple blossoms covered with snow—grief—which she cannot shake off; in the fourth stanza she is compared to a mountain hollow, which is always covered by shadows and where nothing can bloom; and the final stanza continues the previous simile by comparing the melting snow and grief: like the waters which pour forth from the mountains into the dark hollow, thus "grief from everywhere" pours into her "poor heart." This accumulation of concrete images which displace each other creates only a vague, psychological image of the beloved. The same features can be found in the poem "It is not the wind blowing from high," where the poet describes his beloved through a series of nature images. It starts with a negative comparison; it is not the wind that is

touching the leaves on a moonlit night, but the beloved, touching
the poet's soul. The soul is tremulous like the leaves, and multi-
stringed like the *gusli,* and the touch of his beloved is as light
as floating flower petals, as light as the breath of a May night.
Again, there is only a general impression of tenderness and
kindness that lacks any corporeal outlines. The most frequent
device of Tolstoy's poetry is the emphasis of sound over visual
imagery. This occurs in so many poems that it is impossible to
enumerate them all. It may be remembered that in his love poem
"In the midst of a noisy ball" the poet describes the beloved primarily through the sound of her voice, which is likened to "the
sound of a distant reed-pipe" and to the "playful wave of the
sea." Throughout the poem he returns to the sound of her voice:

> A smekh tvoi, i grustnyi i zvonkii
> S tekh por v moem serdtse zvuchit . . .

> And your laughter, sad and ringing,
> Keeps resounding in my heart since that time . . .

and:

> Ia vizhu pechal'nye ochi,
> Ia slyshu veseluiu rech'

> I see the sad eyes,
> I hear the gay speech . . .

In late poems such as "There are many sounds" ("Est' mnogo
zvukov"), "I fell asleep" ("Ia zadremal"), "As soon as I remain
alone" ("Lish' tol'ko odin ia ostanus' s soboiu") and many others,
sound images play a decisive role. In the poem, "There are many
sounds," the poet speaks of the songs of his heart which are
being silenced by the hostile force of life:

> No zhizn' shumit kak vikhor' lomit bor,
> Kak ropot strui, tak shepchet serdtsa golos . . .

> But life is noisy like a storm breaking a fir forest,
> Like the murmur of a brook, thus whispers the
> voice of the heart . . .

Tolstoy's "Impressionism" in his lyric poetry is combined with
pronounced melodiousness. A great number of Tolstoy's poems

are constructed on one model, that of a dialogue with the beloved, for example. But he also uses this form in some of his other poems ("To Aksakov," "To Markevich"). These dialogues usually have one syntactic pattern which consists of an address by the poet, which is followed by questions and/or exclamations. In some poems the pattern is reversed; the poem starts with a statement and is then followed by an address or exclamation. In the love lyrics this pattern is furthermore frequently connected with negation: many of the exclamations or exhortations are negative ("Oh, don't try to restrain your troubled spirit!"). These features indicate a certain general parallelism of sentence structure. This is especially strong in Tolstoy's early poetry. But even in his later poetry, there is syntactic repetition, even if it is not the most dominant feature "Oh, if you only could" ("O, esli b ty mogla").

Tolstoy's language in his lyric poetry may be said to have two variants: a "high" style with Church Slavonic vocabulary,—often combined with complex metaphoric images, and inverted word order; and a "simple" style with colloquial language and simple word order. The former style is less prevalent and occurs primarily in some of his philosophical poems, in some reflective poems, and in a few love lyrics. The majority of Tolstoy's lyric poems are "simple" in terms of formal devices. Tolstoy does not attempt to coin new or unexpected tropes. Most of his metaphors and similes are traditional, taken from the realm of nature, such as the images of the sea, lake, or rivers as metaphors for the poet's love or thoughts.

The images of the ocean and the boat occur as metaphors of life and the poet's fate (cf. the poem "Malice did not persecute us"/"Nas ne presledovala zloba"/; or, the ocean stands for the poet's soul, as in "The waves rise like mountains" ("Vzdymaiutsia volny kak gory"). Another metaphoric image is that of love as a storm (cf. the poem "Into my soul, filled with insignificant vanity"/"Mne v dushu polnuyu nichtozhnoy suety"/). The image of a tree representing either the poet or his beloved also occurs in some poems (cf. "With a sharp axe"/ "Ostroiu sekiroiu"/; "Listening to your tale"/ "Slushaia povest' tvoiu"/; "O friend, you are wasting away your life"/ "O drug, ty zhizn' vlachish'"/).

Tolstoy's similes are also often connected with nature. The most prominent example of similes is in the poem "You are a victim of life's troubles" ("Ty zhertva zhizeneykh trevog") where the beloved is compared to a torn leaf, to smoke, to flowers of an apple tree, and so on. The poet compares his soul to tremulous leaves (cf. the poem "It was not the wind blowing from high"/ "Ne veter veia s vysoty"/), the voice of his beloved to the murmur of the sea (cf. "In the midst of a noisy ball"/ "Sred' shumnogo bala"/), sadness to a thunderstorm (cf. the poem "O, if you only could"/ "O esli b ty mogla"/).

The effect of Tolstoy's poetry does not depend on elaborate figures, except in a few poems. It is rather the combination of simple and common words with a pattern of repetition which accounts for the musicality of Tolstoy's poetry. Syntactic repetition has been already mentioned. To this must be added the use of anaphoras. Tolstoy's favorite anaphora is the connective "and" (i), recurring in a great number of poems. One example is in the poem, "To Aksakov" ("Aksakovu") where sixteen lines (out of a total of fifty-six) start with "i." In Tolstoy's early verse there are also definite attempts at sound effects. For example, in the early poem, "A fir forest," there is not only syntactic repetition, but also quite noticeable assonance, built on the predominance of the vowel u. In his later poetry this is less pronounced, although Tolstoy often begins his poems alliteratively.

IX Technical Aspects of Tolstoy's Poetry

Tolstoy's early poems were written predominantly in ternary meters. His preference lay with the amphibrach, and the relative monotony of the ternary meter was well suited to the melancholy mood of these poems. At that time Tolstoy's metrical pattern had not yet become crystallized. He experimented with short metric forms, such as the two-foot iamb and the two-foot amphibrach; he also used long lines—the six-foot iamb, the hexameter. Of the binary meters, Tolstoy used the iamb and the trochee almost equally, preferring the former in his love poetry, while using the latter for more "extravert" and descriptive poems. In his later verse Tolstoy shows a clear preference for binary meters, mainly the six-foot and four-foot iambs. The former especially becomes his favorite, and is the meter of his love poems, as well as of his other late poems. The four-foot iamb was used primarily in the "Crimean Sketches." The trochee becomes much less important in the late period, and when it is used (as in some poems of the "Crimean Sketches") it is associated with a cheerful, and at times, jocular mood.

Tolstoy's name is also associated with the widespread use of "new" rhymes—inexact rhymes which had been considered impossible in the early nineteenth century. In this respect Tolstoy was not so much an innovator as a continuator of Lermontov (cf. his statement in *Life*, p. 30). Because Tolstoy used a greater number of inexact rhymes in general, his poetry created the impression of having a "daring" rhyming technique. From the vantage point of the twentieth century, however, his rhymes hardly seem unusual.

In essence, Tolstoy's inexact rhymes concerned two major categories of rhyme: so-called truncated rhymes (with the truncated *j*) and unstressed end-vowels. Truncated rhymes belong to his favorites and can be found even in his juvenile poetry. In general, Tolstoy's rhymes are illustrative of the tendency to search for new rhymes, characteristic of the poets of the second half of the nineteenth century, which culminated with the Symbolists' complete destruction of traditional rhyme techniques.

CHAPTER 4

Ballads, Byliny, *and Parables*

TOLSTOY'S second important poetic genre, after his lyric poetry are his ballads. This essentially Romantic genre had been imported into Russia from Germany by Zhukovsky: in 1808 his ballad "Lyudmila" (an adaptation of Bürger's "Lenore") appeared, resulting in a veritable craze for it. Subsequently Zhukovsky wrote more than thirty ballads, adaptations and translations of Schiller, Uhland, Goethe, Southey, and Scott. With the general decline of poetry in the 1830's, the ballad, too, went into eclipse. Tolstoy's ballads represent a revival of the genre, although he eventually changed its character.

Tolstoy's earliest ballads belong to the late 1830's and early 1840's. In the late 1850's Tolstoy wrote a group of poems in folk style which he termed parables. In the late 1860's Tolstoy again turned to the ballad, producing some of his most outstanding works. Since in some of the ballads the poet used *bylina* imagery, he termed them *byliny;*[1] however, there is no essential distinction between them, and in fact they represent works of one genre.

I *Early "Horror" Ballads*

Tolstoy's early ballads were inspired by the examples of Zhukovsky and Lermontov. They are either "horror" ballads in which strange and supernatural events take place or they are Romantic ballads on the theme of oblivion and the transitoriness of glory. The motif of supernatural transformation occurs in three of Tolstoy's earliest ballads, "The Stormy Steed" ("Vikhor' kon'"), "The Wolves" ("Volki"), and "The Tale about a King" ("Skazka pro korolia"). In "'Stormy Steed" a dead horse becomes mysteriously alive on St. John's Eve and gallops through the night until the first cock crows. In "The Wolves" there is a terrifying procession of nine wolves—who in reality are nine ugly, old witches—through a sleeping village. In "The Tale about a

80

King" a righteous, kind king is transformed by a wicked monk into a deer, but eventually regains his humanity. Some awkward metrical switches and occasional grammatical mistakes betray the inexperience of the author; Tolstoy did not include these ballads in any collection of his poetry.

Tolstoy's most "horrible" early ballad is "How the horn owl" ("Kak filin")—inserted in the story "The Vampire"—which is the key to the strange events that take place in it. Set in medieval Hungary, it tells of murder, pillage, fire, and a curse of madness and vampirism that is to be perpetuated from generation to generation: an unfaithful wife lets her lover, the knight Ambrosius, enter her castle with his retinue and murder her old husband and all inhabitants. The dying husband curses her and all her descendants, including in his curse the wish that "a grandmother suck out her granddaughter's blood" (which nearly happens to Dasha in the story). Like the other early ballads, it is written in an uneven, joggling meter, and suffers from an excess of gory details, and somber, but somewhat unclear, symbolism.

II *Romantic Ballads*

Somewhat better and more interesting ballads are the "The Mound" ("Kurgan") and "Prince Rostislav" ("Kniaz' Rostislav") which treat the theme of oblivion, although here, too, Tolstoy is hardly original. In "The Mound,' the poet describes a solitary hill in the steppe under which a famous knight lies buried. When he died, the priests killed all his wives and his favorite horse as sacrifices, while singers promised him eternal glory. However, time passed and obliterated his name and deeds. In the first version of the ballad, the shadow of the knight appears near the tomb, sighing for his lost glory—quite like the image of Napoleon in Lermontov's poem "The Aerial Ship" ("Vozdushnyi korabl' ");[2] the metrical pattern (three-foot amphibrach) of Lermontov's poem is also used by Tolstoy.

In "Prince Rostislav" Tolstoy for the first time uses history which later becomes the principal source of inspiration for his ballads. Yet, the Chronicle story about the fate of the Russian prince who drowned in the Dnieper River is only a poetic pretext, for the ballad is again connected with the theme of oblivion and the "Napoleon motif" of Lermontov's poem. Lying on the bottom of the river, Rostislav calls to his wife, his brother, and the Kievan priests (cf. Napoleon's call to his soldiers, his marshals, and his son). But his voice is feeble, and besides, he has been long forgotten. The image of the nymphs who comb the curls of the drowned prince and kiss him connects the ballad with Lermontov's famous poem "The Nymph" ("Rusalka"), and with Heine's ballad "König Harald Harfagar." There is even textual similarity between Tolstoy's and Heine's works. Nevertheless, it is one of Tolstoy's most charming early ballads, which effectively combines narrative interest with formal smoothness and melodiousness.

III   The "Moscow" Ballads

Only with his "Moscow" ballads did Tolstoy begin to show some originality, as well as interest in history as such. The ballads "Prince Mikhaylo Repnin" ("Kniaz' Mikhailo Repnin"), "Vasily Shibanov," and "The Governor of Staritsk" ("Staritskii voevoda") are all based on episodes from the time of Ivan the Terrible as presented in Karamzin's *History,* and coincided with Tolstoy's work on his novel, *Prince Serebryany.*

In "Prince Mikhaylo Repnin" Tolstoy tells the story of the murder of the prince who refused to humiliate himself by dancing before the Czar in a fool's costume (cf. the mention of this episode in *Prince Serebryany,* and the analogy to Morozov's fate). Repnin accuses the *oprichnina* of vile deeds while nevertheless toasting the Czar. Ivan murders him in a fit of rage, but soon regrets his rash deed and bemoans his "faithful servant." It is an early example of Tolstoy's colorful, bright ballads (cf. pp. 93-94), with partial utilization of *bylina* devices, as for example the description of a feast at the beginning and end.

"The Governor of Staritsk" was written later than the two other "Moscow" ballads and shows greater sophistication in rhythm (Tolstoy uses the six-foot iamb with caesura) and imagery. But the story is again that of the murder of a noble by the terrible Czar: Ivan dresses his victim in his own regal gown, gives him his scepter, and places him on the throne. And then, having royally amused himself, he pierces his victim with a knife, while a "snake-like" smile plays on his lips.

Of the three "Moscow" ballads, "Vasily Shibanov" is the most famous and has become a stock ingredient of any Russian anthology of verse. Based on the story of Prince Kurbsky's defection to the Lithuanians as narrated by Karamzin, its real hero is the lowly servant of the prince, Vasily Shibanov. It is he who helps the prince to escape; it is he who returns to Moscow to hand to the Czar his master's insulting letter written during a sleepless night:

> I pishet boyarin vsiu noch' naprolet,
>   Pero ego mestiiu dyshit,
> Prochtet, ulybnetsia, i snova prochtet,
>   I snova bez otdykha pishet,
> I zlymi slovami jazvit on tsaria,
>   I vot uzh, kogda zanialasia zaria,
> Pospelo emu na otradu
>   Poslanie, polnoe iadu . . .

> And the boyar writes all night long,
>   His pen breathes vengeance,
> He reads, smiles, and reads again,
>   And writes again without resting,
> And with malicious words he taunts the Czar,
>   And, when dawn has appeared,
> He has finished, to his pleasure,
>   A message, filled with venom . . .

The Czar is infuriated by the insolence of Kurbsky and punishes him through Shibanov: he pierces his foot with a staff and throws him into prison, where he is tortured. Shibanov dies, forgiving his master and glorifying "holy, great Russia." No doubt, it was both its patriotic motif (as in *Prince Serebryany*), and its easy flowing rhythm and sonorous language which endeared the ballad to the readers.

A patriotic, and even a "social" motif (directed against the pernicious effect of alcohol on the people!) also occur in two early ballads, "The Night before the Attack" ("Noch' pered pristupom") and "The Knight" ("Bogatyr'"), both of which, however, are of slight artistic value.

IV *Parables and Folk Ballads*

Tolstoy's parables were written about the same time that the poet was writing his folk songs and are similar to them in the use of folk language and tonic verse. They usually tell a story which has a stated or implied moral. For example, the parable "Truth" ("Pravda") speaks about the ambiguity of truth: seven brothers ride out into the world to search for it, and each of them sees it in a different shape. Returning home they begin to argue whose truth was the right one and end up by fighting and killing each other. To the same type as "Truth" belong such parables as "If only the Volga river would run backwards" ("Oi, kaby Volga-matushka vspiat' pobezhala"), and "Vanity goes around" ("Kho-dit Spes'"). The first poem expresses a series of human wishes, such as "if one could start life anew," and "if we could love and never cease loving," concluding with the more specific wish that the Czar may know all the truth. In the second poem the foolish-ness of vanity is presented in the shape of a blown-up, over-dressed creature less than a foot tall, with a hat that is seven feet high.

Tolstoy's short "flirtation" with Askahov and the Slavophiles found its most poignant expression in the poem "Czar, our father" ("Gosudar' ty nash batiushka"), written on the model of a folk song. It consists of a series of questions by a feminine character (possibly, the symbol of Russia) to Peter the Great. The Czar is presented as cooking a thick, salty gruel (*kasha*), which he had imported from abroad, and which he is preparing for posterity. Under this transparent guise Tolstoy was satirizing Peter's stiff Westernizing innovations which had far-reaching results well into the nineteenth century. The poem was very much in vogue with the Slavophiles, since it implied criticism of Peter the Great. Later on, Tolstoy came to denounce the poem and regretted having written it.

The last poem written in folk style was "Panteley the Healer" ("Pantelei-tselitel'"), also written on the model of a popular song. Although it was composed in the 1860's in its form it is similar to the earlier parables, and especially to the poem about Peter the Great. Panteley, a popular saint and healer, is seen walking through the fields, collecting herbs in order to heal suf-ferers. He greets the "good herbs" and swings his stick against "evil herbs." A parallel is then drawn to human society: like evil herbs there have recently appeared people who "cannot stand the sound of *gusli*," and who want to annhilate everything that they cannot "weigh or measure." Against these, the poet says to

Panteley, do not spare your stick! The poem was Tolstoy's first polemical ballad directed against the nihilists and their utilitarianism, and resulted in an uproar in the radical camp.

V *The Polemical Ballads*

Tolstoy's late ballads—they amount to seventeen—written between 1866 and 1873, are without a doubt his best. Now his main source of inspiration became old, medieval Russia; however, Tolstoy used history in different ways in these ballads; as a pretext for polemics on contemporary or past events; to express his own (Westernizing) views on early Russian history; as a decorative background in his "lyrical" ballads.

To the first group belong such ballads as "Against the Current" ("Protiv techeniia"), "A Ballad with a Tendency" ("Ballada s tendentsiei"), "Dragon Tugarin" ("Zmei Tugarin"), and "The Knight Potok" ("Potok Bogatyr'"). "Against the Current" is interesting as a bold protest against the prevalent current of materialism and utilitarian approach to art. Tolstoy makes an appeal to his fellow artists not to surrender, despite their small numbers, comparing their position to that of the image worshipers vis-à-vis the iconoclasts in Byzantium and to that of the Apostles versus the Scribes in the times of Christ. He believes that "the infinite will triumph over the finite" and that one day they will turn "the current" by their faith and devotion to beauty.

However, Tolstoy's preferred means of attack was through humor, and his "Ballad with a Tendency" is one of his most spirited and funny ones. Its comical effect is derived from the unexpected combination of old Russian imagery and vocabulary with modern ideas and terms. A young girl and her beloved, both dressed in old Russian dress, are walking in a beautiful garden and telling each other of their love. The poetic tone is preserved until the seventh stanza, when the prosaic word "turnip" is suddenly dropped. The young man informs his beloved that their beautiful garden with its flowers, bushes, and trees will be soon destroyed: turnips will be planted instead, while a part of the garden will become a pig pasture. What will happen to the nightingale which awakens us every morning with its singing, asks the shocked girl, and is told:

No solov'ev, o lada,
Skoree istrebiti
Za bespoleznost' nado!

But the nightingales, O dear,
Have to be destroyed soon
Because of their uselessness!

When the enraged maiden inquires about the name of those
people who want to destroy everything, she is told that they have
many names: they are "demagogues" and "anarchists" who want
to bring about "equality" and "general bliss." The only remedy
against them would be to hang the "order of Stanislav" on the
necks of their leaders, thus making them into loyal citizens.
The ballad ends with the poet's pretended acceptance of "realism," and his ironic dedication of the poem to the "Russian
Commune."

Tolstoy considered the ballad "Dragon Tugarin" one of his
best. It is the first poem in which Tolstoy presents an idyllic
picture of Kievan Russia at the time of Prince Vladimir. The
title is derived from the *bylina* image of the monster Tugarin
Zmievich (a reworking of the figure of the Polovtsian Khan Tugor
of the eleventh and twelfth centuries) who occurs in the *bylina*
"Alyosha Popovich." Tolstoy uses some *bylina* elements: e.g.
the description of a splendid feast, with which the poem begins
and ends; the *bylina* heroes Alyosha Popovich, Dobrynya Nikitich, and Ilya Muromets who are present; the threefold threats
to Tugarin by the heroes. However, apart from this the ballad
is quite "literary." The poet used the metrical pattern of Pushkin's famous "Song about Oleg the Wise" ("Pesn' o veshchem
Olege") and chose a refrain and vocabulary which were impossible from an "ethnographic" point of view.[3] Tolstoy's main aim
was to present a poetic polemic with Muscovite Russia—a heritage
of the Mongolian Dragon Tugarin. The poem starts with a
description of a splendid feast at Vladimir's court in Kiev. The
Prince wants to have some entertainment and calls for a singer.
Suddenly Tugarin appears—an ugly creature with Mongolian
features. He prophesies that Kiev will go up in flames, while
Vladimir's descendants will become servants of his (Tugarin's)
descendants; that a khan will rule over Russia, and when he
finally disappears, a Russian ruler will become khan instead.

... I vot, naglotavshis' tatarshchiny vslast',
Vy Rus'iu ee nazovëte!
I s chestnoi possorites' vy starinoi,
I predkam velikim na sorom,
Ne slushaia golosa krovi rodnoi,
Vy skazhete: "Stanem k variagam spinoi,
Litsom povernemsia k obdoram!"

And then, having absorbed enough Tatarism,
You will call it Russia!
And you will reject your honorable past,
And putting to shame your great ancestors,
Not listening to the voice of kindred blood,
You will say: "Let's turn our back on the Varanghians,
Let's turn our face to the East!"

But, the ballad ends on an optimistic note. Tugarin is chased away by the heroes, while Vladimir rejects the prophecy and expresses his belief that Russia will eventually overcome all its difficulties.

Another illustration of the theme of "Moscow versus Kiev" is the ballad "The Knight Potok," which earned Tolstoy considerable popularity—and notoriety—at the time of its publication. It is one of Tolstoy's last polemical ballads, appearing in 1871. Like some of Tolstoy's other outstanding works of the 1870's (the satirical poem "The Dream of Popov" and the narrative-inverse *The Portrait*), "The Knight Potok" is written in octaves and has a strong humorous undertone which is interwoven into an essentially serious subject. The *bylina* hero, Potok, one of the oldest Russian epic figures, underwent many strange adventures and was often the victim of witchcraft; this was probably the reason why Tolstoy chose him for his hero. In the poem he is mysteriously transported through time and space from the court of Prince Vladimir, to seventeenth-century Moscow, and then to nineteenth-century Petersburg.

At the feast of Prince Vladimir, Potok outdances everybody else by virtue of his grace and strength. Night falls; the Prince, his family, and his retinue leave the feast; but Potok continues to dance. With colorful strokes Tolstoy creates a fairy-tale atmosphere which precedes Potok's strange experiences:

Vot uzh mesiats iz-za lesu kazhet roga,
    I tumanom podernulis' balki,

Vot i v stupe poekhala baba-iaga,
  I v Dnepre zapleskalis' rusalki,
V Zadneprov'e poslyshalsia leshego voi,
Po koniushniam dozorom poshel domovoi,
  Na trube ved'ma pologom mashet,
  A Potok sebe pliashet da pliashet . . .

The moon is already showing its horns from behind the forest,
  And the ravines are covered with fog,
The witch is already riding by in a mortar,
  And the mermaids are splashing in the Dnieper,
Beyond the Dnieper the howling of the forest goblin is heard,
And the brownie is making his round of the stables,
  On the chimney the witch is waving with a scarf,
  But Potok keeps dancing . . .

Finally he falls asleep from exhaustion, and when he awakens
he finds himself in Moscow five hundred years later. In contrast
to the popular Kievan ruler, the czar of Moscow is seen riding
through the streets with executioners at his side, while the
populace prostrates itself before him. In answer to Potok's
amazed question a passer-by explains that this is their "God
on earth" who "deigns to execute somebody." "We honored our
princes, but not like this," Potok muses, and soon falls asleep
again only to awaken in nineteenth-century St. Petersburg. Here,
Tolstoy satirizes the liberal jury, the materialists, the populists,
and even the emancipated women. A multiple murderer who
"poisoned his father, killed a couple of aunts" and "strangled
two brothers and three daughters" is found innocent by the jury:

"Khot' ubil," govoriat, "ne vinoven ni v chem . . ."

"Although he killed," they say, "he is not guilty of anything . . ."

Potok then sees "an apothecary" lecturing to the people on the
fact that there is no soul and that if God exists, he is "only a
form of oxygen." The hero is sternly questioned whether he
esteems the peasant who is "great by his humility," and who
alone is called to rule the land. Potok's answer—"I esteem the
peasant if he does not squander his crop on drink"—causes an
uproar from which the hero saves himself by flight, musing on
the people's strange need for worshipping—first the khan, now the
peasant. After a final encounter with short-haired, bespectacled

women who are arguing about "some women's rights," Potok
falls asleep. What he will see when he awakens some two hundred years later, the poet says, is open to question. Among Tolstoy's polemical ballads "Potok" is one of the most profound in
thought, and excellent in formal execution.

VI "Norman-Russian" Ballads

The second group of Tolstoy's late ballads, expressing the poet's
"Westernizing" views, is relatively large. To it belong his
"Norman-Russian" ballads, "The Song about Harold and Yaroslavna" ("Pesnia o Garal'de i Iaroslavne"), "Three Battles" ("Tri
poboishcha"), "Haakon the Blind" ("Gakon Slepoi"); some "patriotic" Slavic ballads, such as "Roman of Galizia" ("Roman Gal-
itskii"), "Borivoy," and 'Rugevit'; and the beautiful "Russian
Byzantine" ballad, "The Song about Vladimir's Campaign against
Chersones" ("Pesnia o pokhode Vladimira na Korsun'").

Tolstoy found the subject for "The Song about Harold and
Yaroslavna" while working on his last tragedy, *Czar Boris.* "I
chanced upon a well-known but little exploited episode, namely
the marriage of Yaroslav's [the Wise, 1019-54] daughters, which
made me write the attached ballad," Tolstoy wrote to Markevich.[4] The fact that three of Yaroslav's daughters were married
to European monarchs was a theme well suited to Tolstoy's
views. The ballad tells of the wooing of the Kievan princess
Yaroslavna by Harold of Norway, who is at first refused, but
then accepted after he has proven his valor in battle. But it is
not only a political ballad, it is a ballad about all-conquering
love and spring, written in a "major key," with strong rhythmic
movement and colorful descriptions. A contrasting, tragic "pendant" to it is "Three Battles," which also illustrates Russia's connection with the West.

The poet presents three battles—the Battle of York, the Battle
of Hastings, and a Russian battle against the Polovtsians on the
Dneiper—as taking place simultaneously.[5] A prophetic dream
heralding disaster is seen by the wife and daughter-in-law of
Prince Izyaslav. However, they are unable to avert the tragedy,
and the ballad concludes with the laments of the widows and
children of the slain. The image of ravens who come flying from
the three battle-fields, and tell of the deaths of the warring

princes, give the ballad its specially sinister tone. A somewhat
later "Norman" ballad, "Haakon the Blind," shows the Norwegian
Prince Haakon fighting on the side of his Russian brother-in-law,
Prince Yaroslav.

"Roman of Galizia" is a short, but formally interesting and so-
phisticated ballad. It is based on an episode from Karamzin's
History, in which a legate of Pope Innocent III came to the Russian prince to offer him papal protection. This protection, which
implied some recognition of the Pope, is refused in the poem by
Roman with a polite and dignified speech.

Another "patriotic" ballad is "Borivoy," set in an earlier period. It describes a crusade by German princes in the twelfth
century against the pagan Baltic Slavs. The valiant Slavic chief,
Borivoy, attacks the Germans on the sea and defeats them completely; the formerly proud Germans run in terror and later offer
up fearful prayers to God. In its obvious ironic treatment of the
Germans, at times crude vocabulary, and monotonous rhythm, it
is one of Tolstoy's weakest late ballads.

A "pendant" to "Borivoy" on the theme of pagan Slavs is "Rugevit." Rugevit is the pagan god of the inhabitants of the island
Ruga (Rügen) who is destroyed after Prince Vladimir attacks
the island. But there are also echoes in the ballad of the Chronicle
narrative of the destruction of the pagan god Perun in Kiev,
after the conversion of Russia. The ballad is written in the first-
person form, as if by one of the inhabitants of the island, and
shows an interesting psychological transformation from faith in
the god, to skepticism and indifference:

> I, probudias' ot pervogo ispugu,
> My ne nashli byloi k nemu liubvi
> I razoshlis' v razdumii po lugu,
> Skazav: "Plyvi, v bede ne spasshii Rugu,
> Dubovyi bog, plyvi sebe, plyvi!"

> And, awakening from our initial fright,
> We did not find our former love for him
> And thoughtfully went our way along the meadow,
> Saying: "Swim, oaken god, who did not save Ruga
> In the hour of peril, go, swim!"

One of the longest, and most colorful ballads is "The Song
about Vladimir's Campaign against Chersones." It is based on the

Chronicle story of Russia's conversion to Christianity and consists of two parts. The first describes Vladimir's incursion on Chersones as a means of obtaining the hand of the Byzantine princess Anna; it is written in a humorous tone. The second part describes the return of Vladimir with his bride to Kiev and is purely lyrical in character. The main emphasis in the poem is on Vladimir and his spiritual transformation from an aggressive pagan to a man conscious of his Christian mission. Vladimir's message to the inhabitants of Chersones in the first part is extremely funny in its pseudo-humility:

> ... Sdavaites', proshu vas smirenno,
> Ne to, ne vzyshchite, sob'iu vashu spes'
> I gorod po kamniam razmykaiu ves'
> Krestit'sia khochu nepremenno!
>
> Give yourself up, I humbly beg you,
> Otherwise, don't be angry, I'll kick low your pride,
> And will take the city apart, stone by stone,
> For I want to be baptized by all means ...

The spiritual rebirth of Vladimir in the second part is underlined by a picture of spring which the poet paints in glowing tones:

> Vse zvonkoe ptatstvo letaet krugom,
> Likuiuchi v tysiachu glotok,
> A kniaz' mnogodumnym poniknul chelom,
> Svershilsia v moguchei dushe perelom—
> I vzor ego miren i krotok ...
>
> All the noisy bird-folk are flying around,
> Jubilating in a thousand voices,
> While the prince bent his thoughtful head,
> In his powerful soul a transformation took place,
> And his glance is peaceful and humble ...

VII *The Late Lyrical Ballads*

Tolstoy's late lyrical ballads are among his best. The historical background now becomes incidental to creating a lyrical atmosphere, a poetic mood. This is the case in "Ilya Muromets," "Matchmaking" ("Svatovstvo"), "Alyosha Popovich," "Sadko," "Kanut," and "The Blind One" ('Slepoi").

The ballad "Ilya Muromets" was considered to have veiled autobiographical overtones in the image of the *bylina* hero Ilya Muromets, who is presented as leaving the court of Prince Vladimir, since he feels superfluous. "It's stifling in Kiev, like in a box," he mutters and departs into the woods which smell of "leaves and strawberries." The charm of the poem lies in its naïve diction and formal simplicity, and the glorification of the simple, free life.

The ballad "Matchmaking" was, as the poet himself admitted, only a pretext for speaking about spring and love. Against the background of Kievan Russia, the poet speaks of the wooing of Prince Vladimir's two young daughters by the *bylina* heroes Churilo Plenkovich and Dyuk Stepanovich. The men come to the court of the Prince in disguise and conduct their wooing through lengthy allegorical speeches. The Prince recognizes them, but keeps up the pretense and questions them according to custom. The obvious happy ending and the gay refrain make the ballad one of the merriest which the poet wrote.

In "Alyosha Popovich" Tolstoy returns to the theme of song, while the image of the *bylina* hero who captured a beautiful princess is only incidental. The poet seems to emphasize the mystery of song i.e. poetry and the ultimate impossibility of defining it with words: "Who will understand a song?" the poet asks, and presents a series of images that are evoked by it.

To the theme of song and the singer is also devoted Tolstoy's last ballad "The Blind One": a blind singer has been invited by a prince and his retinue to amuse them while they rest in the forest. However, by the time the old man arrives, they have gone to continue their hunt. The blind singer does not realize this and sings his song as if he had listeners. Only toward the end does he realize that he is alone. Yet he is not bitter about it—for he must sing whether anyone hears him or not. The ballad ends with the singer's greeting to all—to the forest, the spring, the stars which heard his song, to the prince, the boyars, and the people who did not hear him. The ballad is an impressive praise of the power of song and re-echoes the ideas expressed in *John Damascenus*.

Tolstoy's ballad "Sadko" is—in the poet's own words—a *"Situationsbild"* and conveys only a mood. From the *bylina* of the Novgorodian hero, Sadko, and his strange adventures and travels, Tolstoy picked out only one episode: his stay at the castle of the king of the sea. The king wants to keep Sadko for ever, and offers him the rank of councilor and even one of his daughters as wife. But Sadko is tormented by longing for the earth which he envisages in the beauty of spring. The high point of the ballad is the dance of the king of the sea to the accompaniment of Sadko's *gusli,* which causes a storm that ruins many ships and sailors. Realizing what he has done, Sadko breaks the strings of his instrument, but is chased out of the sea by the enraged king. He returns to earth, where nobody believes his tales.

A tragic theme is counterbalanced by a picture of spring and beauty in the ballad "Kanut": the young Danish prince Kanut receives an invitation from his cousin Magnus who plots to murder him. Simultaneously, Kanut gets a letter from his wife who warns him of Magnus and tells him of an evil dream which she had. But Kanut is happy and trusting and disregards her words, just as he disregards several omens that he encounters on the way. He rides through the beautiful spring landscape, intoxicated by the song of birds, the murmur of the sea, and the smell of wild roses—into the arms of death. The theme of life and death has nowhere been as poignantly expressed as in this ballad, and despite Kanut's inevitable ruin, life seems to be triumphant.

In a letter to Markevich Tolstoy wrote: "When I look at myself from the side (which is rather difficult) then it seems to me that I can characterize my work in poetry as being in the major key, which sharply distinguishes [it] from the prevalently minor key of our Russian poets, with the exception of Pushkin, who is definitely in the major key."[6] Although this statement does not apply to Tolstoy's lyric poetry, it is quite justified in regard to his ballads, especially those of the late period, for they are characterized by opulent settings, bright landscape and character descriptions, and gaiety and élan.

Tolstoy likes to present sumptuous feasts, and to describe rich clothing. This can already be found in such early ballads as "Prince Mikhaylo Repnin" where the feast of Ivan the Terrible is presented as follows:

> Kovshami zolotymi stolov blistaet riad,
> Razgul'nye za nimi oprichniki sidiat.
> S vecherni l'iutsia viny na tsarskie kovry,
> Poiut emu s polnochi likhie gusliary . . .

The row of tables sparkles with golden goblets,
Reveling *oprichniki* are sitting at them
From the evening mass on, wines pour over the imperial rugs,
Since midnight wild singers are singing for him . . .

In the later "Moscow" ballad, "The Governor of Staritsk," the poet describes in great detail the rich garments with which Ivan clothes his enemy; and one of the final accents in the poem is the "embroidered boot" with which the Czar steps on his murdered victim. In the later ballads, such as "The Song about Harold and Yaroslavna," "The Song about Vladimir's Campaign," "The Knight Potok," and even in the "Ballad with a Tendency" decorative settings contribute significantly to the brightness and joyousness. For example, Harold's return to Norway after his marriage to Yaroslavna is presented in bright, colorful terms:

Tsvetami ego korabli obvity,
Chervlennye bereg pokryli shchity
I s chernymi vranami stiagi.
V lad'iakh otovsiudu k shatram parchevym
Prichalili veshchie skal'dy . . .

His boats are covered with flowers,
The shore is covered with red shields
And with banners with black ravens.
From all sides the wise skalds
Are arriving toward the tents made of brocade . . .

Probably the most colorful ballad is "The Song about Vladimir's Campaign," and in it, especially the presentation of the arrival of the Byzantine princess. The mention of gold, diamonds, pearls, silks, and brocades make the setting seem like a firework of colors. In his "Ballad with a Tendency" Tolstoy gives an elaborate description of the old Russian dress of his main characters, also creating a highly comical contrast to the modern ideas which they discuss.

Nature, too, is bright and gay. In nearly all ballads describing nature, Tolstoy inevitably stops on his favorite season—spring. It is spring in "The Song of Harold and Yaroslavna," in "The Song about Vladimir's Campaign," in "Matchmaking," in "The Ballad with a Tendency," in "Ilya Muromets," in "Alyosha Popovich," in "Kanut," and in "Sadko." One of the most beautiful depic-

tions occurs in "Kanut" as the young Danish prince rides through
the land to his fateful encounter with Magnus:

> V"ezzhaiut oni vo trepeshchushchii bor,
> Ves' polnyi vesennego krika,
> Gremit solov'inyi v shipovnike khor,
> Zvezditsia v trave zemlianika.
> Cheremukhi vetvi dushistye gnut,
> Vse dikie iabloni v tsvete. . . .

> They ride into the trembling forest,
> Filled with spring sounds,
> The choir of nightingales sounds in the sweetbriar,
> Wild strawberries stand like stars in the grass.
> The bird cherry trees bend their fragrant branches,
> All the wild apple trees are in bloom. . . .

The atmosphere of spring is connected with love and youth.
The heroes of the ballads are young, handsome, and noble. Such
are Vladimir in "The Song about Vladimir's Campaign," the
two heroes in "Matchmaking," Harold of Norway, Alyosha Popovich, the Slavic chief Borivoy, Sadko, Kanut, Roman of Galizia.
Tolstoy imbues them with a spirit of chivalry that makes them
appear like medieval knights. Thus Vladimir, the aggressive and
impetuous pagan, is moved to kindness and generosity at the
sight of his beautiful bride; Harold of Norway departs to distant
lands with the name of Yaroslavna on his lips and later presents
his whole kingdom to her. In similar manner, the two heroes in
"Matchmaking" cannot forget Vladimir's daughters and return
from their exile to woo them; Kanut, who does not believe in the
treachery of Magnus, seems to personify trust and nobility;
and even Alyosha Popovich, who kidnaps the princess, woos
her with music and song like a troubadour. Tolstoy's love and
affinity with the Romantic Middle Ages left their imprint on
his ballads.

The formal pattern of Tolstoy's ballads is somewhat distinct
from that of his lyric poetry in that binary meters are used less
frequently than in his lyric poetry. The six-foot iamb, which
became Tolstoy's favorite meter in his late lyric poetry, is used
only in two relatively early ballads ("Prince Mikhaylo Repnin"
and "The Governor of Staritsk") and in the late ballad "Rugevit";
the four-foot iamb is used in "The Ballad with a Tendency"

and "Matchmaking"; while the trochee appears in "Borivoy," "Ilya Muromets," and "Alyosha Popovich." Tolstoy's preference in his ballads lies with the four-foot amphibrach—possibly due to the model of Pushkin's "The Song about Oleg the Wise," influences of which can be discerned in "The Song about Vladimir's Campaign." Eleven of Tolstoy's late ballads are written in this form, and among them are some of his best: "Dragon Tugarin," "The Song about Vladimir's Campaign," "Sadko," and "Kanut."

The prevalence of a certain rhythm creates a predominant mood, and in the case of the ballads, it is primarily a joyous mood. Folk-song devices, such as parallelism of construction, fixed epithets, and especially refrains, which in combination with the other elements, create an impression of gaiety. Thus, Tolstoy's ballads complement admirably his melancholy and subdued lyric poetry and manifest another side of the poet's artistic personality.

CHAPTER 5

Humorous and Satiric Poetry

TOLSTOY'S predilection for humor is noticeable in some works of his early prose, in a few lyric poems, and in some ballads; the distribution of certain poems into the category of "ballads" rather than "humorous poetry" or vice versa seems artificial and arbitrary at times.[1] What remains unchallenged, however, is the fact that Tolstoy was one of the outstanding representatives of humorous poetry among Russian poets of the nineteenth century. His humorous talents unfold themselves most effectively in the poetry of "Kozma Prutkov" and culminate in the daring satiric poem, "The Dream of Popov."

The tradition of Russian humorous and satiric poetry is, of course, an old one, dating back to Kantemir's satires and Sumarokov's satirical odes in the eighteenth century. In the early nineteenth century the Arzamasians[2] used parodies, epigrams and satires in their fight with the Archaists. Satire and parody became an even more clearly polemical weapon in the hands of radicals of the 1860's. Poets like Minaev, Veinberg, Kurochkin, and even the radical theoretician Dobrolyubov, parodied the adherents of "pure art"—Fet, Maykov, Polonsky, Shcherbina, and others. It was in this atmosphere of flourishing parody that Tolstoy wrote his humorous and satiric poems.

A clear adherent of "pure art," Tolstoy fought back against the nihilists and radicals. Yet they were not his only target, for often his barbs were directed at the extreme right as well. He would also bring out ridiculous elements in the works of his fellow artists. Often his humor transcended the purely temporal and topical and turned to themes of eternal triviality. Finally, he was a master of nonsense verse, such as had not yet existed in Russian literature.[3] This breadth of Tolstoy's humor distinguishes him to a considerable degree from his contemporaries.

Tolstoy's humorous poetry must have been more voluminous than what is extant. Problems of censorship prevented the poet from printing many of the poems during his lifetime, and he was not particularly careful in preserving them. Some have been saved only because Tolstoy inserted them in his letters; others, however, have been irrevocably lost. The recent Soviet edition prints thirty-five poems, some of which were written in cooperation with the Zhemchuzhnikovs.

Although Tolstoy's humorous and satiric poems are quite diversified, they can be divided into roughly three categories: nonsense poetry, parodies, and polemical poetry. Occasional poetry, and "medical" poems make up the first category; a number of poems by "Kozma Prutkov" belong to the second; and longer poems and ballads, with some definite "point," such as "Russian History" make up the third.

I *Nonsense Poetry*

Tolstoy's nonsense verse is virtually untranslatable, since very often the poems have no literal meaning; their humorous effect is achieved by illogical contrasts and plays on language. For example:

> Zheltobriukhogo Gavrilu
> Oblivali molokom,
> A Malan'ia govorila:
> On mne vovse ne znakom . . .

> They poured milk
> Over yellow-bellied Gavrila,
> While Malanya kept saying:
> I don't know him at all . . .

There is no logical connection between the nonsensical action presented (why pour milk over Gavrila? why is he yellow-bellied?) and Malanya's comment, and this makes for the comic effect of the lines.

Tolstoy's "medical" poems were written in the late 1860's (1868-70), and their hero was Tolstoy's doctor, A. I. Krivsky, who treated the poet at Krasny Rog. There were apparently more poems of this type than have been preserved. Some of the "medical" poems are "The doctor to the lady bug" ("Doktor bozhiei korovke"), "The dung beetle" ("Navoznyi zhuk"), "The doctor and the sexton" ("Vrach' i ponomar'"), "The birch hut"

("Berestovaia budochka"), and "The Spanish fly" ("Mukha shpanskaia"). Most of the poems are pure nonsense verse and derive their effect from paradoxical situations and play with language. As an example, the first poem describes a nonsensical situation—a rendezvous between the doctor and the ladybug which has erotic overtones. In "The dung beetle" the doctor's poisoned wife, Adolphina, returns to scare him at night in the shape of a dung beetle. "The doctor and the sexton" is the story of a nonsensical bet: the sexton assured the doctor that hard-boiled eggs turn to amber in the stomach. The doctor being of a "skeptical character" and "disliking the clergy," swallows five hundred eggs to disprove the sexton's point—and dies. The same nonsensical content characterizes the other "medical" poems.

II *Parodies by "Kozma Prutkov"*

A special place among Tolstoy's light poems is occupied by the poetry of "Kozma Prutkov"—the joint production of Alexey Tolstoy and Alexander and Vladimir Zhemchuzhnikov. Already in the late 1840's and early 1850's the cousins had produced a comedy, *Fantasy,* a parody on lowbrow comedy. The plot of the piece was centered on the wooing of the young ward of an old, rich woman by various suitors who were promised her hand if they could find the old woman's lost pet dog, Fantasy. The play evoked the displeasure of Emperor Nicholas I and was not published until 1884. At about the same time that they wrote *Fantasy* the cousins embarked on another satirical venture under the guise of a fictitious author, "Kozma Prutkov"—a ridiculous, pompous bureaucrat, an incarnation of mediocrity. Tolstoy's part in all of "Kozma Prutkov's" works has not been fully determined; however, it has been found that certain poems were written by Tolstoy in collaboration with Alexander Zhemchuzhnikov, others with Vladimir Zhemchuzhnikov, and still others by Tolstoy himself. Most of the poems are parodies: either on anthological poetry written by different contemporary poets or on Romantic poetry glorifying the exotic (e.g., Spain), or on the numerous imitations of Heinrich Heine that were popular in Russia at the time.

The parodies on anthological poetry make fun of some poets'

exaggerated infatuation with the "classical Greek." This is indi-
cated by some of the titles and subtitles of the "Prutkov" poems,
such as "An ancient plastic Greek" ("Drevnii plasticheskii
grek"), which, incidentally, is an epithet of a live being and
not of a piece of sculpture, as might be expected; "To an ancient
Greek old woman" ("Drevnei grecheskoi starukhe") is the title
of another poem; "From the ancient Greek" ("S drevne-greches-
kogo") is the subtitle of the poem "A philosopher in a bath"
("Filosof v bane"). At times, the parodies refer to specific poets
and their works. Thus the poem "A letter from Corinth" ("Pis'-
mo iz Korinfa") parodies N. Shcherbina's poem, "A Letter"
("Pis'mo").

Among poems on the "Spanish theme," "The Desire to be a
Spaniard" ("Zhelan'ie byt' ispantsem") and "The Siege of Pamba"
("Osada Pamby") are noteworthy. The first poem parodies the
conventional presentation of wild, Spanish amorous passions.
"The Siege of Pamba" is considered to be a parody of Zhukovsky's "Fragments from the Spanish Romances about Cid"
("Otryvki iz ispanskikh romansov o Side"), as well as Katenin's
"Romances of Cid" ("Romansy o Side").[4] The siege of the castle
of Pamba by the "Castilian Lion" Pedro Gomez and his army is
made ridiculous by their vow not to touch any food except
milk. After a siege of nine years the army retreats with tottering
knees but in the proud consciousness of having kept their vow.

In the parodies on Heine, or rather, on his epigones, the
nonsensical element, and the unclear, ambiguous situations which
are often present in Heine, are stressed. In the poem "The leaves
wither, summer passes" ("Vianet list, prokhodit leto") Junker
Schmidt wants to shoot himself—for reasons unknown to the
reader. The poet exhorts his hero not to do it, for summer
will return, although there is no evident connection between
the passing of the seasons and Junker Schmidt's plight. In the
poem "Near the sea, close to the city gates" ("Na vzmor'e, u
samoi zastavy") there is a parody on a Romantic, tragic (and
completely unclear) love situation: while a gardener is sadly
watering his asparagus and cabbage one day, an official in
"warm galoshes" drives up to him in a *troyka* and asks for his
daughter. The gardener only hopelessly waves his hand; the
official rides back, and the gardener follows him with his eyes,
morosely picking his nose.

III   *Poems with a "Point"; Polemical Poems*

Tolstoy was fond of writing humorous epistles to his friends; some of them are light and playful; others contain, at times, a serious point. To the light poems belong the epistles to Arnoldi and Dmitri Tsertelev. The former is one of the last which Tolstoy wrote; during his last stay in Florence in March, 1875 the poet received a package of biscuits (*sukhari*) from his friend, Mikhail Petrovich Arnoldi. He replied with a poem of pure nonsense, written, however, in an elevated, solemn language. Tolstoy expresses his happiness over the gift and orders his "frivolous stomach" to sing "a daily canon of praise" to its sender. Tolstoy's political moderation is nowhere as clearly seen as in the short epistle to his nephew, Prince D. N. Tsertelev, which starts with the lines:

> Boius' liudei peredovykh,
> Strashusia milykh nigilistov . . .
>
> I am afraid of progressive people,
> I fear the dear nihilists . . .

For a man who was as clearly and fundamentally opposed to the nihilists as was Tolstoy, the use of the term "dear nihilists," even though ironically, was an indication of the elegant moderation which he could nevertheless preserve in these matters.

Tolstoy's epistles to Feofil Tolstoy were written on a serious matter which was of great importance to the poet; specifically, the discussion of his tragedy, *Czar Fyodor*, by a special commission which was to decide on its suitability for the stage. Feofil Tolstoy, as a member of the commission, cast his vote against the presentation of the tragedy, although admitting to its high artistic qualities. Apparently he had written to the poet on this subject, and Tolstoy's epistles were replies to him. In the first epistle Tolstoy humorously accepts Feofil's reasons for rejecting the tragedy and apologizes for his "near-sighted" reproach. In the second, Tolstoy rejects Feofil's praise of his work—a comparison with Shakespeare and Lessing. "Why compare a hill with / Mount / Aetna?" he asks. And continuing the comparison with Lessing's "Laokoön" he makes a subtly ironical comment:

Ne mniu, chto ia Laokoon,
Vo zmei upershiisia rukami,
No skromno zriu, chto osazhden
Lish' dozhdevymi cherviakami . . .

I don't imagine that I am Laokoon
Grasping the serpents with my arms,
Rather, I perceive with modesty that
I am besieged just by earth worms . . .

The epistle to Longinov, although phrased in a playful tone, is more serious. It was written as a defense of Darwin whose books were attacked by some extreme conservatives. Longinov, a friend of Tolstoy and chairman of the censorship committee, was apparently inclined to agree with the conservative side. Tolstoy in his poem argued persuasively for the freedom of science, while at the same time aiming a good kick at the nihilists who, he said, only perverted Darwin's theory. Tolstoy's argument is, interestingly enough, based on a religious point of view: God's ways, in science as in other things, cannot be known to a mere "chairman of the censorship committee," and such thinking may even "smell of heresy a bit." The last stanza which switches from an elevated glorification of science to colloquial speech is rather funny, since it paraphrases one of "Kozma Prutkov's" nonsensical aphorisms—"Esli u tebia est' fontan, zatkni ego!" ("If you have a fountain, plug it up!"):

Bros' zhe, Misha, ustrashen' ia:
U nauki nrav ne robkii,
Ne zatknesh' ee techen'ia
Ty svoei driannoiu probkoi . . .

Stop, Misha, your threats:
Science is not fearful in nature,
You cannot plug up its course
With your wretched cork . . .

Some of Tolstoy's longer poems continue the line of his non-sense poetry, although they usually have a certain point. One of the most famous of these is the poem "Rebellion in the Vatican" ("Bunt v Vatikane") which treats the subject of the Pope's castrati who are doomed to eternal celibacy and singing.[5] The castrati decide one day to rebel against their more fortunate master, and want to subject him to their fate. The Pope is frightened, and swiftly calls for his minister, who quiets the castrati by bringing his soldiers. Tolstoy introduced the names of two important church figures into the poem: Cardinal Antonelli and the minister of the Vatican, Merode, both of whom were alive at the time. The Pope is likewise identified as Piux IX. This factor, together with some vulgar lines, made it impossible to print the poem in Tolstoy's lifetime.[6]

On the borderline between nonsense poetry and polemical poetry stands "The Ballad about the Chamberlain Delarue" ("Ballada o kamergere Delariu")—possibly a satire directed against the idea of non-resistance to evil.[7] The chamberlain Delarue (who, despite his name, is Russian) is stabbed by a villain. However, instead of resisting him, he lifts his hat and politely thanks him. This initial nonsensical action is followed by a series of others, each more absurd than the other: Delarue invites the villain to his home for "a cup of tea," promises him the order of Stanislav, one hundred thousand rubles, and even the hand of his daughter Dunya. The reaction of the villain is an example of brilliantly portrayed psychology showing that "a spoilt heart" cannot accept "good for evil." Murdering his benefactor with a poisoned dagger, the villain robs Dunya of her honor "in the attic" and flees to Tambov where he soon becomes a "much-beloved" governor. Returning ultimately to Moscow, he becomes a member of the Senate and then of the Imperial Council. The poet stops here before the promotion of his hero leads him into too high government circles. The final lines of the poem are contained in a purposefully ambiguous tone, making it unclear whether the poet praises or condemns the development of this affair.

Tolstoy's polemical poems are less numerous than his nonsense poems, but they belong to some of his best. His preoccupation with contemporary problems found its reflection in such poems as "Unity" ("Edinstvo"). In it Tolstoy satirized the ultra-reactionaries' attempts at forcible Russification of all non-Russian nationalities which had been especially intensified after the Polish rebellion of 1863. Tolstoy presents Katkov, prince Cherkassky, Samarin,[8] and even his friend Markevich in a hypothetical effort at Russification by trying to make Negroes white —if only they existed in Russia. The image of prince Cherkassky

painting the Negroes' faces with white paint, while Samarin
rubs their behinds with chalk is eminently funny, despite the
poem's serious undertone.

Problems of Russia's past history had an even greater attraction
for Tolstoy, and he always returned to them in his various works.
In "The Ballad about a Mandarin" ("Ballada o mandarine")
Tolstoy turns to the theme of "disorder in the Russian land"
which had been repeated since the times of Nestor's *Chronicle*.
Tolstoy presents this theme under the very transparent guise of
Chinese history: the chief mandarin Tsu-Kin-Syn asks his mandarins the reason for disorder in China. The mandarins explain
that this is because of the youthfulness of their country, for they
say: "We are very young—only five thousand years old." The
chief mandarin is dissatisfied with their answer and orders them
all to be whipped. The main effect lies in the name of the chief
mandarin—a Chinese-sounding version of the Russian for "son-
of-a-bitch"—as well as the funny answers of the lower mandarins.

To the same theme is devoted Tolstoy's famous poem "A
History of Russia from Gostomysl"[9] ("Russkaia istoriia ot Gosto-
mysla") which, the poet claimed, had been inspired by Nestor's
Chronicle. However, the humorous treatment of Russian history,
and the language of the poem which consists of very colloquial
Russian, with occasional insertions of German and French phrases
far remove it from its alleged model. Only the constant refrain
"Still there is no order" is derived from the *Chronicle,* and at the
very end of the poem Tolstoy suddenly switches to Church
Slavonic which, however, only adds to the humorous effect of
the whole. Tolstoy traces the development of Russian history
from the Varangians to the nineteenth century, by representing
a series of portraits of Russian rulers. Some are drawn in a
humorous, nonsensical vein, others with a satiric point. Thus
the Varangian founders are presented as "three middle-aged
brothers"; Vladimir who baptized Russia "died from grief" since
he had not been able to create order; Ivan the Terrible was
called thus because he was "a serious, solid man"; Boris Godunov,
"a brunet, and not bad looking" nearly brought order to Russia
when the Pretender overpowered him; a number of stanzas
are devoted to Peter the Great, in which Tolstoy's Westernizing
views are apparent, for although some of Peter's measures were
strict, he writes, he nearly managed to bring stability to Russia.

Peter's successors receive a less kind treatment: Empress Elizabeth was "a gay monarch" who loved to sing and to be merry—but there still was no order; Catherine's flirtation with Voltaire and Diderot and with ideas of freedom ended with "attaching the Ukrainians to the land"; and Alexander I had "weak nerves," but was nevertheless "a gentleman." For obvious reasons Tolstoy could not draw humorous portraits of later monarchs, and instead he switches to the various ministers who had played important roles in the nineteenth century. The poem ends with an address to Timashev, the current Minister of the Interior, with the plea that he may finally restore order. Despite certain restraint which the poet had to exercise in his satire, "A History of Russia" is memorable for its gaiety and wit.

IV *"The Dream of Popov"*

Tolstoy's best and boldest political poem is "The Dream of Popov" ("Son Popova"). With its 336 lines written in octave form, it is a worthy counterpart to the late narrative-in-verse, *The Portrait*. Such is the mastery of the poet that despite its very obvious political implications the poem remains a work of art.

The poem starts *in medias res* with a strange dream which Councilor Popov had: he sees himself going to congratulate a minister on the latter's nameday, in dress uniform, but without trousers. When he notices his "deshabillé" it is too late, for he is already in the antechamber of the Minister. The image of Popov is comical, yet quite credible: a distant cousin of "Kozma Prutkov," he belongs to the type of uninspired, naïve, and servile bureaucrat whose main thought is advancement in his career. His first reaction to his terrible discovery is one of shock. But then he remembers that the minister is known for his liberalism, so he takes heart and begins to think that the situation may be even turned to his advantage:

> A chto, podumal on, kol' moi nariad
> Ponravitsia? Ved' est' zhe, pravo slovo,
> Svobodnoe, prostoe chto-to v nem!
> Kto znaet? Chto-zh? Byt' mozhet? Podozhdem!

> But what, he thought, if my appearance
> Will be found pleasing? There is indeed

> Something free, simple about it!
> Who knows? Well? Perhaps? Let's wait!

The portrait of the minister is a masterpiece of political satire. A gentleman with "elegant manners" and a "friendly face," he likes to convey the image of a liberal, and therefore appears in informal dress rather than in uniform. His speech to his subordinates is contained in high-flowing generalities and clichés which are similarly intended to convey his liberal views: "I am a servant of the people," "my ideal is complete freedom," "we must ... hand the reins of government ... to the people," and so on. The final part of the speech, devoted to the future of Russia, is a splendid piece of nebulous rhetoric.

When the minister spots Popov and asks him to appear before him, the latter is still torn between "hope and doubt." But when the minister sees Popov's scant attire, his former friendliness goes over into a crescendo of fury, while he bombards Popov with questions: What prompted him to take off his pants? Was he born in Scotland? Or had he possibly read too many novels by Walter Scott? Or was he trying to depict a Roman patriot? Or could he possibly dare to symbolize the Russian budget? And in an amazing switch to arbitrariness, he accuses Popov of plotting to overthrow the government and hands him over to the Third Section (The Imperial Secret Police).[10]

Popov is taken to "the beautiful house known for its just judgments" where a benevolent-looking colonel begins to interrogate him. And the methods of the secret police, which start with "gentle persuasion" and end with threats, have a frightening air of contemporariness. Despite the fact that Popov assures the colonel that his only crime consisted in forgetting to put on his pants, he finally gives in, and writes a long confession of his crime implicating a large number of friends and acquaintances.

The poem ends, however, on a light note. Popov wakes up to find that he is lying in his bed, while his pants are hanging with his uniform on a chair. "It was only a dream! O joy! O happiness!" he exclaims. The rest of the poem is devoted to alleged arguments by the reader who cannot believe in the story. The reader questions the possibility of such accusations as were leveled at Popov. He cannot imagine such a minister, a demagogue in Russia (even if they may exist in goodly numbers in France!), he has never heard of the institution to which Popov was taken. The crime itself seems unlikely—who ever heard of a person forgetting to put on his pants? But the poet cuts short these arguments with the ingenious reply:

> Ia ne Popov! Ostav' menia v pokoe,
> Rezon li v etom, ili ne rezon.
> Ia za chuzhoi ne otvechaiu son . . .

> I am not Popov! Leave me in peace,
> Whether there is rhyme or reason in it or not.
> I cannot answer for somebody else's dream . . .

Of all of Tolstoy's humorous poems, "The Dream of Popov" occupies the foremost place by its wit, lightness, and elegance of language and form.

CHAPTER 6

Translated Poetry

TOLSTOY'S interest in translations was sporadic and marginal, since his original work occupied most of his energy. Occasionally, however, he liked to test his abilities as a translator. In the 1850's he undertook some translations of Chénier, Byron, Herwegh, and Heine; in the 1860's he translated a few more poems by Heine and two ballads by Goethe.

I Early Translations: Byron and Chénier

Tolstoy's earliest translations are two poems by Byron: the famous lyric "The Destruction of Sennacherib," based on the Bible story of the siege of Jerusalem by the Assyrian King Sennacherib; and the Romantic, melancholy poem "Sun of the Sleepless." The first poem must have appealed to Tolstoy by its somber dramatism and biblical language, while the theme of longing over the past in the second was quite in tune with Tolstoy's own poetry. Besides, Fet was also translating "Sun of the Sleepless" at the same time, so there was a certain amount of poetic competition involved. "I would like to see whether my translation is better or worse than Fet's," Tolstoy wrote to his wife.[1] Although Tolstoy's knowledge of English was probably weaker at the time than his knowledge of French and German, his translations are very fine, and remarkable in conveying the imagery and rhythm of the originals. Two lines show this:

> For the Angel of Death spread his wings on the blast,
> And breathed in the face of the foe, as he pass'd . . .

> Angel smerti lish' na veter kryl'ia proster,
> I dokhnul im v litso, i pomerknul ikh vzor . . .

Although Tolstoy had some moral reservations about some of Chénier's poetry, which he considered too "free," he saw in the poet a genuine "painter and artist" and felt "real pleasure in translating [him] ... a tangible, plastic pleasure; a pleasure of imagery which permits one to devote oneself entirely to the music of verse."[2] Tolstoy's translations of Chénier consist of six bucolic poems, "Tiré de Moschus," "C'est le dieu de Niza," "Accours, jeune Chromis, je t'aime," "L'impur et fier époux," "Fille du vieux pasteur," and "A compter nos brébis." However, most of the translations are rather free, both in terms of content and in form. Thus, the eight lines of the original "Fille du vieux pasteur" are lengthened to fourteen lines by Tolstoy; the six lines of "Accours, jeune Chromis" become ten lines in Tolstoy's version. The metrical patterns of Chénier were not preserved either, and all poems are written in six-foot iambs. These "inaccuracies" are probably due to Tolstoy's enthusiasm for Chénier, which lead him only to conveying the general tone and outlines of the French poet's poetry. And although Tolstoy's own poetry is free from Chénier's influence, in a few poems of the "Crimean Sketches" there are traces of the plastic and colorful vision of the world which characterized the French poet.[3]

Tolstoy soon turned to German poetry and remained with it from then on. His favorite poet was Heine, with whom he shared a love of humor and irony, even though he did not share Heine's skepticism. "I have re-read Heine and find that he is a real poet, a remarkable poet—and extremely original. How could he have been a wicked person? A feeling of malice, hatred, and even the lowest feelings can be found in his works next to the most elevated and poetic feelings," Tolstoy wrote to his wife.[4]

The second important poet for Tolstoy was Goethe. At one time Tolstoy toyed with the idea of translating *Faust* and even started on it; however, this plan was never realized, although some important elements of *Faust* went into the creation of *Don Juan*.

One of Tolstoy's earliest German translations was Herwegh's poem 'Ich moechte hingehn wie das Abendrot," which in its mystic tone was close to Tolstoy, but Tolstoy never again returned to the works of this poet, and the poem seems to have provided simply the impulse for a nearly original poem by Tolstoy. The eight lines of the original grew to twenty four lines, and the affirmative, quiet tone of Herwegh's poem formed only the first part of Tolstoy's poem. In the second part, the

poet developed the idea of the disharmonious death of man—
in contrast to nature's quiet death—which is not to be found
in the original. This peculiar ending is especially noteworthy
since it is one of the rare examples of Tolstoy's vision of dis-
harmony in the universe.

II *Translations from Heine and Goethe*

Tolstoy's most numerous translations, however, stem from
Heine. Even some of Tolstoy's original poems—his lyric poems
about the sea (e.g., "The sea moves"), as well as some of his
humorous poems show the influence which the German poet had
on Tolstoy. Among the poems by Heine which Tolstoy translated were: "An den Nachtwaechter" (the last stanza), "Es ragt
ins Meer der Runenstein," "Die schlanke Wasserlilie," "Mein
Liebchen, wir sassen beisammen," "Nun ist es Zeit," and "Koenig
Richard." In most of the poems Tolstoy reproduces Heine's
imagery and tone with accuracy and fine feeling. Thus, the
lyrical tone of "Die schlanke Wasserlilie" is perfectly captured
in the Russian version, which even preserves small details of
the original (diminutives, some epithets). The same sensitivity
to tone and imagery can be found in such poems as "Mein
Liebchen, wir sassen zusammen" ("Obniavshis' druzhno, sideli")
where the final lines of the translation seem to convey the image
of the sea at night even better:

> A my—bezuteshno my mimo
> Po temnomu moriu plyli . . .

> Wir aber schwammen vorueber
> Trostlos auf weitem Meer . . .

Sometimes Tolstoy permits himself some slight formal liberties.
In Heine's poems, "Es ragt ins Meer ein Runenstein" and "Nun
ist es Zeit" Tolstoy uses the amphibrach throughout (Heine
alternates it with the iamb). But the tone of nostalgia in the
first poem and of tragedy in the second are preserved faithfully
in the Russian versions. Tolstoy's final lines which bring in the
image of the gladiator (Heine uses the image of the fencer) in
"Nun ist es Zeit" are probably even more dramatic. Tolstoy
translated only one of Heine's ballads, "Koenig Richard," one

of his best translations; in its tone of gaiety it somewhat resembles Tolstoy's late ballad, "Kanut."

Tolstoy's most impressive translations are from Goethe. He translated two of Klaerchen's songs from *Egmont* ("Freudvoll und leidvoll" and "Die Trommel geruehret") and the ballads "Der Gott und die Bajadere" and "Die Braut von Korinth." The latter two are especially interesting since they are the only two examples of long translations undertaken by Tolstoy. They also seem to form an introduction to Tolstoy's original ballads which began to appear in quick succession during the following year (1868).

Tolstoy's preoccupation with the supernatural throughout much of his artistic work no doubt attracted him to Goethe's ballads. The theme of "Der Gott und die Bajadere"—the ultimate salvation of a fallen woman through the power of love—had been already expressed in Tolstoy's early narrative-in-verse, *The Sinner.* The vampire theme of "Die Braut von Korinth" had figured prominently in Tolstoy's early prose and ballads. Tolstoy worked very conscientiously on both ballads and was satisfied with his translation. He found the Russian language more beautiful than German and considered that some stanzas had gained in the translation. His principle was "to convey the impression" of the original: "It is necessary that the reader be transferred to *the same sphere* in which the reader of the original found himself, and that the translation affect the same nerves," he wrote to his wife.[5] From the point of view of form, both poems were complicated, yet Tolstoy managed to follow faithfully the patterns of both. If one compares the original and the translation, for example, "Der Gott und die Bajadere," it becomes evident that Tolstoy kept to the text nearly line by line:

> Es freut sich die Gottheit der reuigen Suender
> Unsterbliche heben verlorene Kinder
> Mit feurigen Armen zum Himmel empor...

> Raskaian'e greshnykh liubimo bogami
> Zabludshikh detei ognevymi rukami
> Blagie voznosiat k chertogam svoim . . .

In "Die Braut von Korinth" Tolstoy was somewhat less exact, and complained about the difficulty of the short (two-foot iambic) lines which occurred in every stanza. Nevertheless, the eerie quality of the ballad is conveyed by the poet with great mastery.

Tolstoy's last translation was also a ballad, an anonymous Scottish folk poem, "King Edward," which had been translated into German by Theodor Fontane. Tolstoy worked from this translation, and only later did he discover the original. In a letter to Markevich, Tolstoy expressed his enthusiasm about the simplicity and "beautiful naïveté" of the work. The gruesome patricide by the hero of the ballad is conveyed through a series of questions and answers between him and his mother who, as is revealed in the last stanza, incited him to the deed. Tolstoy's skill in this work and in his other translations is another affirmation of his remarkable poetic gifts.

CHAPTER 7

Narratives-in-Verse

THE popularity of narratives-in-verse (as of poetry in general) had declined considerably since the 1840's when prose assumed a dominant position. Tolstoy's interest in and utilization of this genre once again underlines his connection with an earlier poetic tradition. Tolstoy had definite propensities for larger poetic forms, propensities which found their most impressive realization in his tragedies. His early narratives-in-verse represent, in a sense, his first steps in this direction.

Tolstoy wrote five narratives-in-verse, one of which remained unfinished. The first poem, *The Sinner* (*Greshnitsa*), was written in 1857 and appeared in the Slavophile journal *The Russian Colloquy* in 1858. The second poem, *John Damascenus* (*Ioann Damaskin*), written immediately afterward, appeared in the same journal in 1859. Produced toward the end of Tolstoy's "lyric" period, these two works are thematically and formally connected with Tolstoy's lyric poetry: many of the religious, philosophical, and artistic views which Tolstoy had expressed in his lyric poems were enhanced and broadened in them, while the emphasis on lyricism gave them their peculiar coloring. The unfinished poem, *The Alchemist* (*Alkhimik*), was probably written in the early 1860's, and was published in Tolstoy's only lifetime edition of poetry in 1867. It shows some thematic connection with the dramatic poem *Don Juan,* which Tolstoy was writing in the late 1850's and early 1860's; its formal elements connect the poem with Tolstoy's lyric poetry.

In the 1870's, after having completed the dramatic trilogy, Tolstoy again turned to narratives-in-verse. The poem *The Portrait* (*Portret*) was written during the winter of 1872/73 and appeared in *The Messenger of Europe* in 1874. The last poem, *The Dragon* (*Drakon*), conceived during the spring of 1872 in Italy, was finished in 1873 and published posthumously in the

113

same journal in 1875. In contrast to the early "lyric" poems, Tolstoy stressed the narrative interest in his late poems and used a more "prosaic" diction. Thematically, too, the late poems are quite distinct from *The Sinner* and *John Damascenus*. Tolstoy returned to the Romantic, fantastic themes of his early prose stories and to a clear expression of the "l 'art pour l 'art" principle which he came to champion increasingly from the 1860's on.

I   The Sinner

The Sinner is Tolstoy's shortest work in this genre: it consists of only about two hundred lines. Written approximately at the same time as such religious-philosophical poems as "In the land of rays" and "I, who in darkness and dust," it takes its subject from the New Testament. Although the religious element never disappeared completely from Tolstoy's work, it was especially strong in the late 1850's and coincided with the poet's Slavophile connections. In St. Luke, 7:37, an episode is described in which a sinful woman is converted through her encounter with Christ. Tolstoy took the Gospel story as a basis for his poem; however, he elaborated and dramatized it, making it into a conflict between the woman and Christ which ends with the miracle of conversion.

The poem starts with the presentation of a sumptuous feast in a rich house in Palestine during which the guests converse on various subjects. Finally they turn to the discussion of a strange man who teaches humility and forgiveness and whose glance "no one has been able to withstand yet." A beautiful courtesan who overhears the conversation is tempted by pride to challenge publicly the powers of the stranger. Her challenge is answered soon, for a man "bright as God's archangel" approaches the crowd. The woman gets up from the table and with a cup of wine in her hand taunts the stranger. It turns out, however, that she has made a mistake, for the stranger is John of Galilee, not Christ. Christ follows him, humble and simple. He does not speak but only fixes his eyes upon the woman. Silence falls upon the crowd as the two stand opposite each other. But suddenly, a miraculous conversion takes place in the woman's heart. She understands with horror the wickedness of her life, and, crying bitterly, she falls at Christ's feet.

Dramatic effectiveness, one of the most prominent features in the poem, is emphasized by picturesque details; the image of the feast set in an exotic, luxurious setting is evoked twice. A whole section is devoted to the description of the beautiful sinner, dressed in transparent silks and adorned with gold and diamonds. Yet the concomitant result of this picturesqueness is a certain flatness of characters. The heroine of the poem is seen only through her actions, from the outside. John of Galilee and Christ—presented in strongly contrasting terms—do not even utter a word. This lack of any psychological description and the absence of dialogue was noted by various critics, who pointed to the "superficiality" of the work and to the lack of psychological motivation for the sinner's sudden conversion. Although these objections are valid to a certain degree, one must bear in mind Tolstoy's essentially mystic, religious approach. His intent in the poem was to portray a miracle, not to explain it. Two conflicting ideologies—a sensuous, worldly, and an ascetic, other-worldly—are presented. The sinner's words (addressed to John of Galilee) make a persuasive plea for the worldly side of existence:

> . . . Lish' naslazhden'em ia vlekoma,
> S postom, molitvoi neznakoma,
> Ia veriu tol'ko krasote,
> Sluzhu vinu i potseluiam . . .

> I am driven only by pleasure,
> I don't know fasting and prayer,
> I believe only in beauty,
> And serve wine and kisses . . .

The cup of wine which she holds in her hand underlines the sharp confrontation and is simultaneously a symbol of worldly pleasures. Yet, such is the power of Christ that without uttering a word he converts the woman to a new, Christian life.

The poem was written in Tolstoy's favorite form, the four-foot iamb. Despite the occasional use of Church Slavonic vocabulary which enhances the biblical subject of the poem, the overall effect is one of melodiousness and lightness. There is an abundance of pyrrhics, the short line has few enjambments, and frequent anaphoric constructions. The growing tension of the final

moment (Section 6), for example, is effectively underlined by
a series of anaphoras: of the thirty-two lines of this section,
twelve lines begin with the anaphoric *i* (and). Alliterative
effects and assonance are used extensively, and the occasional
use of triple rhyme—relatively rare in Tolstoy's poetry in general—also adds to the melodiousness of the work. Although *The
Sinner* is not outstanding among Tolstoy's poems, the poet himself seems to have retained a special fondness for it, for at his
last public appearance in Karlsbad in July, 1875 Tolstoy chose
this work, which he read to a warmly appreciative audience.

II   John Damascenus

John Damascenus is one of Tolstoy's most memorable poems
in its tone of genuine devoutness and the beauty of its language.
Its melodious qualities attracted P. I. Tchaikovsky (1840-93) and
S. I. Taneev (1856-1915) to put parts of the poem to music. At
the same time *John Damascenus* contained various philosophical
and personal ideas which Tolstoy had expressed in some of his
short lyric poems. It was this latter element which was recognized by the censorship, and which put the publication of the
poem into jeopardy for a while. The general reading public,
curiously enough, also reacted negatively toward the poem which
it found too "worldly" despite its religious subject.

Tolstoy based *John Damascenus* on the legend of the eighth-
century saint's life as presented in the Russian Menologion, the
Chet'yi Minei. From it the poet chose the most crucial point in
John's life: his renunciation of a high position at the court of
the Saracen caliph and his retirement to the monastery of St.
Sabas near Jerusalem.

The poem starts with the description of the opulence of the
court of the caliph where John occupies a position of great honor
and trust. Yet John is unhappy in the midst of all this splendor,
and his desire for a simple life of "work, prayer, and song" drives
him to beg the caliph to let him go. At first the caliph offers
him even greater power and half of his kingdom. But John persists in his request, and realizing his sincerity, the caliph agrees
to his departure. John divides his riches among the poor, leaves
his castle, and starts on his wanderings. Section 2, which contains John's song of blessing as he views the beauty of God's

universe, is one of the most beautiful lyrical passages in the poem. After prolonged wanderings John finally comes to a desert monastery where he is accepted by a stern elder who demands of him a vow of poetic silence as sign of submission and humility. John agrees to this condition despite the suffering which the vow causes him, since his great desire had been to praise God through song. When a monk dies, one of the brethren begs John to compose a song for the dead. Touched by pity, John breaks his vow, and composes a magnificent prayer for the dead (Section 8). In the middle of the funeral ceremony the elder suddenly appears, accuses John of pride, and threatens to expel him from the monastery, but divine interference finally helps John. The Mother of God appears to the elder at night and tells him to stop the persecution of John and let him sing. The last chapter describes the song of John as he glorifies God and his creation.

The emphasis which Tolstoy gave the legend, transformed the life of a saint into the life of a poet, with art and its freedom becoming one of the main themes of *John Damascenus*. At the beginning of the poem John is already characterized as a fighter against "the mad heresy" which rose against art.[1] While keeping his vow of silence at the monastery, John suffers as an artist who had been denied freedom of creativity. An anonymous narrator intrudes into the poem, saying that "coercion and oppression of free thought" is not pleasing to God. Finally, to lend special emphasis to this idea, Tolstoy puts John's defense into the mouth of the Virgin who tells the elder to "leave his melodies to Damascenus" which she compares to the flowers of this earth.

The elevation of art and the singer had been already expressed in Tolstoy's lyric poetry and were connected with the poet's Romantic, Neoplatonic philosophy. Another idea which found its reflection in Tolstoy's poetry and in *John Damascenus* was the conception of this world as a reflection of a much more beautiful world. This idea is part of John's plea for freedom, and it is the main reason for his rejection of worldly glory. As an artist John can perceive the ideal forms and re-create them, becoming thus an intermediary between the ideal world and reality. When John is requested to compose a song for the dead, he "listened for a long time . . . to the invisible singing" and then "with an obedient hand" wrote down what he had heard.

In addition to the presentation of John as an artist-singer rather than an orthodox saint, the poem had obvious autobiographical features. Not only could Tolstoy's ideas be recognized in the mouth of John, the poet himself seemed to be partly embodied in the figure of the saint. John's high position at the court of the caliph, his description as a champion of art, his dislike of court life and its pomp—all this seemed to be only a slightly veiled representation of Tolstoy's position and feelings at the Court of Alexander II. Tolstoy's desire to be a poet rather than a courtier seems to be echoed in the lines:

> ... Prostym rozhden ia byt' pevtsom,
> Glagolom vol'nym Boga slavit' ...

> ... I was born to be a simple singer,
> To praise God with a free word ...

And John's anguished plea—"O let me go, caliph, permit me to breathe and sing in freedom!"—had a personal ring which could hardly be misunderstood.

To the contemporary reader the controversial side of *John Damascenus* is obliterated by the distance of more than one hundred years. What remains is its lyricism and its simple and devout mood. The lyric, song quality of the poem is achieved by a marked accumulation of melodious devices such as rhythmic variety, alliteration, assonance, parallel constructions, and anaphoras. It is further stressed by the loose structure of the poem. *John Damascenus* consists of a series of poems (12), some of which are quite independent of each other. This independence is marked by the use of various metrical patterns: the four-foot iamb, the five-foot iamb, the hexameter, and the amphibrach. There are a number of remarkable single poems in *John Damascenus*: the first poem describes the court of the caliph and creates a striking pictorial and melodious effect which is rather typical of Tolstoy's early narratives-in-verse. But the focal points of the poem as a whole are the "Song of Blessing" (Section 2), and the "Song of the Dead" (Section 8).

John's blessing, sung after his departure from the court of the caliph, consists of three major themes: at first, John blesses the beauty of this world which evokes inspiration in the singer; then, he begins to search for a worthy topic for his inspiration; finally, he finds an object for his adoration and for his song: it is Christ, not "triumphant in greatness," but again, as in *The Sinner*, mild and humble. In a passionate outburst John regrets that he did not live in the time of Christ and could not suffer with him. One of Tolstoy's favorite devices in the song of blessing is a threefold anaphora—in keeping with the religious tone of the poem:

> Blagoslavliaiu vas, lesa,
> Doliny, nivy, gory, vody!
> Blagoslavliaiu ia svobodu
> I golubye nebesa!
> I posokh moi blagoslavliaiu . . .

> I bless you forests,
> Valleys, fields, mountains, waters!
> I bless freedom
> And the blue heavens!
> And I bless my wanderer's staff . . .

Combined with a simple, unpretentious diction the song builds up to a lyric crescendo of Christian devotion. Perhaps no other poem by Tolstoy reflects so poignantly the poet's adoration of God's universe and his strong religious feeling.

The prayer for the dead forms a striking contrast to the song of blessing. In the former the poet had extolled life and Christ; here, he presents death. The vanity of the world and the inevitability of death for all is the theme of the prayer. It is interesting that the prayer is written in the first-person form and is put in the mouth of the dead monk who calls from the coffin and admonishes the survivors to think of the end. Here, Tolstoy seems to have followed examples of eighteenth-century poetry, and especially Derzhavin's[2] poems on death. The grotesque presentation of death and some lines in the prayer are strongly suggestive of Derzhavin's ode "On the Death of Prince Meshchersky" ("Na smert' kniazia Meshcherskogo"). The sound effect is heavy and gives an excellent reproduction of prayer with its use of Church Slavonic vocabulary, old grammatical forms, and inverted syntax. It shows Tolstoy's amazing facility in using various levels of language in a most striking form.

III   The Alchemist

The Alchemist is a fragment of a little over two hundred lines; it was apparently planned as a fairly long work. The source for the poem was a medieval legend about the seneschal of the Baleares, Don Raimund Lullius. According to the legend, Don Raimund was riding through the streets of Palma in the year 1250 when he saw a beautiful lady, Doña Eleonora, with whom he immediately fell in love. Forgetting all propriety and the fact that he was on horseback, Don Raimund followed her into church. There, not heeding the commotion which he was causing, he made an ardent declaration of love. Doña Eleonora responded with a demand for the elixir of life, since she hoped to get rid of her admirer in this way. Don Raimund accepted her demand, departed for distant lands where he devoted himself to the study of alchemy, and experienced a number of strange adventures.

Tolstoy's poem which consists of three sections, gives only the beginning of the story. It starts with the description of the splendid setting of a church service which is suddenly disrupted by the appearance of a rider. "Who is he?" the people exclaim in indignation. But when they realize that his glance is riveted on one of the ladies in the church, "a whisper of sympathy" passes through the crowd. Don Raimund's ardent declaration of love is answered with restraint and irony by Doña Eleonora. She feels that such passionate love as theirs would be too much for the short, earthly life usually accorded to mortals. "We must become immortal," she says, and asks him to search for the elixir of immortality. Don Raimund swears to do as she asks and departs from his native land. The last unfinished section presents him addressing nature as he sets sail.

The fragment is written in the four-foot iambic meter, with the same melodious devices which Tolstoy used in his earlier poems. The exotic setting at the beginning of *The Alchemist* is suggestive—both in terms of pictorial and sound effects—of the beginning of *The Sinner* and *John Damascenus.* The dramatic appearance of Don Raimund in church, and his confrontation with Doña Eleonora is also reminiscent of the dramatic situation in *The Sinner.* Tolstoy's interpretation of Don Raimund is interesting in that the hero seems to combine the impetuous passion of Don Juan with the thirst for knowledge—and alchemy—of Faust. In the unfinished section he makes a speech in which he tries to comprehend the underlying principle of the universe. It seems probable that Tolstoy left the poem unfinished because he incorporated these elements in the hero of his dramatic poem, *Don Juan.*

IV The Portrait

The Portrait is Tolstoy's longest poem: it consists of six hundred and ninety-six lines. Written toward the end of the poet's life, its subject was "somewhat idyllic . . . a little like *Dichtung und Wahrheit,* reminiscences of childhood."[3] The poem tells, in the form of a first person narrative, of the strange love affair between a shy, little boy and the eighteenth-century portrait of a beautiful lady. The action proceeds rather slowly at the beginning, and is interspersed with digressions by the narrator who is clearly identifiable with Tolstoy. Thus, he satirizes the "barrack style" of contemporary architecture with its yellow paint, which he considers a heritage of Arakcheev,[4] and ultimately of the Tatars. An advocate of "classical" education, the poet expresses the opinion that "exercise of thought" rather than technology and science can further enlightenment. In a playful aside to Stasyulevich, his editor, he apologizes for not being a "realist," and he takes a stab at the "realist" press which has yet to master the Russian language. The main part of the poem is an excursion into the past, which combines nostalgia, humor, and fine psychological insight into adolescent nature:

In an old, aristocratic house in St. Petersburg the hero, a boy of ten or eleven years, lives surrounded by servants, old aunts, and tutors. He is a dreamer who longs for beauty, while reality which he sees around him is repulsive to him. Trying to find a definition for the term "ideal," much-repeated to him by his German tutor who admires Kant, the boy's attention becomes focused on the portrait of a young woman in one of the halls of the house. The picture attracts the boy by its mysterious beauty, and soon he becomes hopelessly enamored of it. Every day after his lessons the boy goes to look at it. His greatest fear is that someone may discover his secret love, and the mere mention of old-fashioned clothes, powder, and "even Derzhavin" is sufficient to bathe him in cold sweat. One day while looking at the beautiful lady the boy gets the impression that she is silently imploring him to rescue her from the imprisonment of her frame. He decides to come back at night—although he nearly oversleeps the rendezvous—and when midnight strikes the portrait comes to life, and the lady steps out of the frame. But now, having rescued his adored lady, he does not know what to do. Her laughter at his awkwardness reduces the boy to tears, and under the conciliatory kiss of the beauty he faints rather comically in her arms. When he recovers his senses, it is broad daylight; he finds himself surrounded by his family and a doctor who are discussing the nature of his illness. The portrait of the lady hangs on the wall as before, and only a faded rose which the boy still clutches in his hand, remains a token of his strange romance.

Tolstoy's skill in blending reality and fantasy had been observed already in his early prose (e.g., "The Vampire"), and in *The Portrait* the strange nocturnal adventure of the boy is presented in great detail so as to stress its verisimilitude. Despite the doctor's diagnosis of "somnambulus" and "febris cerebralis," an intentional ambiguity remains, which makes it equally possible that either the dream was a reality or that reality was a dream.

Tolstoy wrote *The Portrait* simultaneously with "The Dream of Popov," and this apparently influenced the form of the work, for it too, was written in iambic pentameter, in octave form. Tolstoy used two styles in the poem: a "prosaic" and a "romantic." The former is used primarily at the beginning of the poem to describe the setting and is characterized by unpoetic vocabulary (colloquial expressions, foreign words, etc.), and frequent enjambments which create the impression of prose. The "romantic" style is used for the description of the portrait, as well as for the boy's nocturnal adventure. It uses the same devices which had been observed in Tolstoy's early narratives-in-verse: poetic vocabulary, anaphoric constructions, pronounced alliteration, and assonance. The romantic atmosphere surrounding the portrait is enhanced by the mention of flowers and music. A bunch of roses adorns the breast of the lady, and her hands hold an apron filled with roses. In the twilight hour, while the boy would look at her, a street organ would play Mozart's "Cavatina." When the lady finally steps out of the frame, the roses fall at the boy's feet, the whole hall is filled with their scent, and the sounds of a minuet accompany the dance of the lady and the boy.

Despite its clear autobiographical elements, *The Portrait* more than any other of Tolstoy's narratives-in-verse, echoes a number of literary works: Tolstoy's own prose, Perovsky's Romantic tale "The Black Hen" ("Chernaia kuritsa") written expressly for the eleven-year old Tolstoy, Lermontov's "Fairy-tale for children" ("Skazka dlia detei"), and, last but not least, Pushkin's *Eugene Onegin.* The motif of a portrait coming to life had already been used by Tolstoy in "The Vampire," and it is interesting to note that the descriptions of the portraits in the two stories are nearly identical: both represent young girls with powdered hair and roses on their breast. The strange experiences of the ten-year-old hero during a dream in Perovsky's "Black Hen" may also have had some effect on *The Portrait.* But more specific seems to be the influence of Lermontov's fragment—his prosaic beginning, his metrical pattern, and the image of the heroine, a young girl who lives in a world of dreams and fancy in an old house in St. Petersburg. Finally, the model of Pushkin's *Onegin*—a narrative-in-verse, interspersed by various digressions by the author—looms large. The description of the hero's lonely childhood, the humorous portrayal of his education and of his teachers, and the early awakening of love are strongly suggestive of the first chapter of *Onegin.* Some lines, with addresses to the reader, or epigrammatic statements are evocative of Pushkin's work:

> Chitatel' moi, skazhi, ty byl li molod?
> Ne vsiakomu izvesten sei nedug.
> Pora, kogda liubvi nas muchit golod,
> Dlia mnogikh est' ne bolee kak zvuk . . .

> My reader, tell me, have you been young?
> Not everyone is familiar with this illness.
> The time, when thirst for love torments us,
> Is for many nothing but an empty sound . . .

The publication of *The Portrait* was deplored by radical critics as a renaissance of the school of "pure art" which had flourished in the 1850's. Although the poem has hardly any "message,"

the theme of infatuation with beauty that runs through it made
it appear outdated. In retrospect, however, *The Portrait* appears as one of the early symptoms of the poetic revival which
was to inaugurate the Symbolist movement.

V   The Dragon

Tolstoy's last poem, *The Dragon*, with its 580 lines, is slightly
shorter than *The Portrait* and completely distinct from that
poem. It is a seemingly objective narration, yet its subject is
pure fantasy. Tolstoy's aim in the poem was, as he said, to lend
"verisimilitude to an impossible fact"[5]—an aim in which he
succeeded admirably. The poem has the subtitle "A Story of the
Twelfth Century. From the Italian." No Italian original, however, existed; Tolstoy simply wrote this in order to mystify his
readers and critics.

The poem is set during the struggle of the Guelfs and Ghibel-
lines in Italy. Yet, the main theme of the poem is not this historical struggle, but rather the manifestation of the supernatural
in the form of a terrifying dragon. The story is told by the Lom-
bardian armorer, Arnolfo, who fights in the army of the Guelfs
and is sent by his dying commander to Chiavenna to gather
forces for a counterattack on the enemy. Travelling through the
mountains with a young companion, Guido, they lose their way
in the darkness. When dawn comes they find themselves near
a terrible, enormous monster. Guido lightheartedly throws a
stone at the dragon, to prove that it could not possibly be alive.
But the dragon is real and begins a terrifying descent into the
valley where it feasts on the dead bodies lying on the battlefield. When the frightened travelers finally reach Chiavenna,
they find that the city has surrendered to the enemy. A new
attempt to fight ends in final defeat. The tale ends with a curse
on the traitors who called the "German dragon" into the Italian
land, for the terrible vision is recognized as an omen of the
misfortunes which were to descend upon the country as a result
of the internecine wars.

It is difficut to ascertain whether the poem was intended as
an allegory on contemporary political conditions; no doubt,
parallels could be drawn to attempts at Italian unification in
the 1860's and 1870's. However, the patriotic element in the

poem is clearly subordinated to the dramatic presentation of a terrifying vision per se. Various devices are used to stress the verisimilitude of this vision. The poem is written as a frame story: an anonymous narrator describes an old Italian church which contains a baptismal font with the image of a terrifying dragon. Looking at it, the narrator expresses his doubts about the existence of such a beast, but is silenced by the sudden appearance of Arnolfo, who tells of his terrible experience. Arnolfo's narration proceeds slowly and is interspersed with dialogues between him and Guido and with detailed descriptions of the landscape. The monster is revealed gradually: at first the travelers notice it as a battlement through the fog, and think that they have reached a castle. When the fog lifts, they see it as a gigantic statue hewn by an unknown artist. Only after Guido's lighthearted action does the dragon slowly come to life. When it returns to the mountains after having devoured the dead bodies in the valley, it appears again like a statue set against the dramatic background of a setting sun. Thus the dragon has a twofold function in the poem—it is a fantastic "reality" and at the same time a symbol of the misfortunes which visited the country.

As in *The Portrait*, Tolstoy used the iambic pentameter in *The Dragon*. In his rhyme scheme, however, Tolstoy followed the example of Dante's *terza rima*; this feature was to lend further authenticity to this "Italian story." The medieval setting of the poem is underlined by its language, which is archaic and ponderous. Church Slavonic words and forms are frequent, as is the use of inverted word order. There is also a tendency to use colloquial expressions which acquire grotesque, archaic connotations in the context of the poem. The tendency toward prose which was noticeable in *The Portrait* is quite pronounced in *The Dragon*. Its rhythm is less varied, enjambments are frequent, and the sound effects (often based on alliteration) are harsh. Yet this harshness is, at times, magnificently effective, as for example in the final curse of the narrator where Tolstoy utilizes the names of various Italian cities:

> Iz veka v vek vas da klianut v narode,
> I da zvuchat pozorom vekovym
>   Nazvan'ia vashi: Asti, Redzh'o, Lodi!
> Vy, chrez kogo vo prakhe my lezhim,
> Piachentsa, Komo, Mantua, Kremona,

Vy, ch'i usta iz zloby ko svoim
Prizvali v kraj germanskogo drakona!

Let the people curse you throughout the ages,
And let your names: Asti, Reggio, Lodi
Sound in eternal shame!
You, through whom we lie in ruin,
Piacenza, Como, Mantua, Cremona,
You, whose tongues called the German dragon
Into the land, because of malice toward your own [people]!

A poetic tour de force with fantasy ultimately triumphant,
The Dragon demonstrates Tolstoy's poetic virtuosity at its height.

CHAPTER 8

The Dramatic Poem Don Juan

THE idea for *Don Juan* arose in Tolstoy's mind in the late 1850's, and his draft dates from 1859. After some reworking and changes suggested by various literary friends, Tolstoy published the poem in *The Russian Messenger* in 1862. A few months later Tolstoy published a letter in the same journal which was simultaneously a plea for the acceptance of "pure art" and an explanation of his ideas in the poem. Despite this plea, however, *Don Juan* was hardly appreciated and understood in its time; it remained a work "for the few," being overshadowed by Tolstoy's tragedies and his lyric poetry.

I Don Juan Theme

The Don Juan theme is, of course, a rather old one in literature. Starting with its first appearance in the early seventeenth century from the pen of Tirso de Molina, it embarked on a migration across world literature. After having appeared in various Italian variants, *Don Juan* was reworked by Molière, and his *Dom Juan ou Le festin de pierre* exercised an important influence on writers of the seventeenth and eighteenth centuries. But it was with Mozart's opera *Don Giovanni*, and with the Romantics in the nineteenth century that the Don Juan theme found its most numerous reworkings. E. T. A. Hoffmann, Lenau, Grabbe, Byron, de Musset, Balzac, Merimée, Alexandre Dumas-père, Pushkin, and Zorilla were among the many writers and poets who were fascinated by the image of the eternal lover. The work of Zorilla especially, the religious-fantastic drama *Don Juan Tenorio*, with its strong emphasis on the idea of salvation, has been termed "the Don Juan of the nineteenth century."[1] It is quite understandable that as a Romantic Tolstoy found himself attracted to the Don Juan theme. His unfinished narrative-in-verse, *The Alchemist*, had already pointed in that

127

direction. Taking as his point of departure Mozart's opera and E. T. A. Hoffmann's interpretation of it, Tolstoy created one of the few Russian versions of Don Juan.[2]

II *Tolstoy's* Don Juan

Tolstoy's work consists of two parts, preceded by a prologue and followed by an epilogue. The prologue, as in many medieval mystery plays, and in *Faust* (cf. below), deals with a contest between Satan and heavenly spirits concerning the soul of the hero whom each side claims as its own. Satan plans to show to Don Juan the feminine ideal which the latter will search for in vain in every woman.

Part One, which takes place ten years after the action of the prologue, opens at the Holy Tribunal in Seville. Leporello has been caught by the Inquisition, which suspects his master, Don Juan, of impiety. Under threat of torture Leporello gives a report on Don Juan's amorous habits, as well as on his "heretical" religious views, which amount to the belief that "man is free to pray as he pleases" and that "you . . . cannot drive him into paradise with a stick." The Holy Tribunal declares Don Juan a heretic and decides to have him secretly murdered. Don Juan in the meanwhile, is involved in a love affair with Doña Anna to whom—unlike most Don Juan versions—he is officially engaged. In the opening monologue he weighs his feeling for her and for a moment thinks it may be *the* love which he had sought all his life. But then his usual cynicism takes over, and in an impassioned speech he rejects love, honor, conscience, and even—God. A tender encounter with Doña Anna in her room soon thereafter seems to reverse once again Don Juan's mood. The entrance of the Commodore (Doña Anna's father), who asks Don Juan to leave since it is improper for them to stay alone so long, enrages the latter, and he secretly vows to take revenge. The same evening he publicly serenades Niseta, a well-known prostitute. The Commodore who witnesses the scene with Doña Anna is enraged and challenges Don Juan to a duel. Don Juan kills the Commodore and flees.

Part Two takes place about a year later near Cadiz where Don Juan has fled. A papal nuncio is about to arrive in Cadiz in order to urge the Inquisition to be more severe: Don Juan's arrest and trial are unavoidable. He thinks of leaving Spain, but wants to see Doña Anna beforehand. "Let Doña Anna be my last, bitter triumph in Spain," he says to himself. He goes to Seville and stealthily gains admittance to Doña Anna's villa at a moment when patrols are already searching for him. Despite initial revulsion and horror Doña Anna hides him in her room and succumbs to him. When Don Juan leaves her, he feels strangely dissatisfied: "I stole the victory like a thief," he muses. On his way back he challenges the statue of the Commodore to dine with him on the following evening. Returning to Cadiz Don Juan finds that soldiers of the Holy Inquisition have surrounded his castle and want to arrest him. He fools the officer in charge by making Leporello impersonate the papal nuncio, Hieronymus, who orders the soldiers to withdraw. At the farewell feast in Don Juan's castle Doña Anna suddenly appears, asks Don Juan to repent, and leaves. Don Juan becomes thoughtful and suddenly realizes that he loves her: "I am yours, Doña Anna! Come to me! I am yours! Come! I love you, I love you!" he rapturously exclaims. But at that moment the Commodore enters, asks Don Juan to prepare for death, and tells him that Doña Anna has poisoned herself. Don Juan curses everything and falls down dead.

In the first—and more complete—version (as opposed to the 1867 edition) Satan appears and claims Don Juan's soul, but the heavenly spirits rescue Don Juan, and keep him alive for he has finally known love. When Don Juan regains consciousness on the following morning, he realizes his terrible guilt and his loss. He decides that he must go on living in order to expiate his sins and retires to a monastery.

The epilogue takes place in a monastery near Seville, many years later. Don Juan does not appear in it any more, and is only discussed by the abbot and a monk who speak of his mortal illness and praise his exemplary humility during his life in the monastery. The epilogue ends with the prayer of the monks for Don Juan's soul.

Goethe's *Faust* and Hoffmann's "Don Juan" are the two works that most influenced Tolstoy's dramatic poem. There are clear parallels to *Faust* in the prologue (the praise of God and his creation by the good spirits, the contest between Satan and the heavenly forces, the idea of the hero's ultimate salvation),

in the humorous and ironic portrayal of Satan, and in Don
Juan's striving for the eternal feminine ("*das Ewig-Weibliche*")
which makes him akin to Faust.[3] Hoffmann's influence is seen
in Tolstoy's characterization of Don Juan and Doña Anna. For
Hoffmann was "the first who saw [in Don Juan] the searcher
for an ideal and not simply a reveller."[4] According to Hoffmann
there were two stages of development in Don Juan: at first he
believes in love, but after having been disappointed many times,
he turns into a skeptic. This conception, adopted by Tolstoy,
made his hero a disappointed idealist rather than a sensualist
and rogue. His striving for love is a search for "the source of
all truths," for "the hidden origin of all phenomena," in other
words, for a basic existential philosophy or faith. His inability
to find love makes him for a while into a rebel against society
and its institutions, especially the Church. Yet in this conflict
with the Church, Tolstoy's Don Juan occupies the position of an
enlightened skeptic vis-à-vis narrow fanaticism. Thus, he is
tolerant of other faiths "as long as they pay tribute to the king,"
generous and forgiving toward enemies, and cosmopolitan.[5]

The active, fighting Don Juan is only one aspect of Tolstoy's
conception of the Don Juan theme. The poet's idea of love which
he equates with God raises the whole problem of Don Juan
into a religious sphere, in which the hero's soul becomes a field
of contest between good and evil, God and Satan (cf. the epigraph). It is interesting that while Tolstoy argues for God, he
makes also a very good case for Satan who is both humorous
and profound. In his arguments with the heavenly spirits, Satan
seems to outshine them by his wit, while some of his philosophical reflections (e.g., on the relativity of truth) are extremely
persuasive. Evil, according to Tolstoy, is a necessity in order to
give man freedom of choice between good and evil. Satan
says in the prologue: "I am the dark background in a painting,
the logical tribute to necessity." Don Juan, in the final analysis,
is free to choose as he likes. The fact that Satan's views are
humanly quite acceptable makes it a difficult choice indeed. The
fact that Don Juan nevertheless chooses love and God, serves
to underline Tolstoy's essentially religious, mystic approach to
the theme.

Traditionally Doña Anna had been assigned a secondary
and passive role in the tragedy of Don Juan. However, this con-

ception underwent gradual change, and in Hoffmann she is an equal to the hero "with regard to the highest favors of Nature . . . a divine woman, over whose pure soul the devil has no power."[6] Tolstoy's Doña Anna follows Hoffmann's version of her and is possibly even a more forceful character. Proud, strong, and impetuous, she does not deign to conceal her feelings and sends Don Juan an impassioned love letter; during their rendez-vous (Part One) she solemnly swears eternal fidelity to him—and keeps her vow until death. Her faith in Don Juan is near-religious. Even after he compromises her and kills her father, she cannot believe that she was mistaken in his character: "No, it was not me whom you deceived, Juan, you deceived God and nature," she says. And when she comes to Don Juan for the last time after having taken poison, she finds a confirmation of her original faith in him through a new, mystic insight which is closed to him. Doña Anna is Don Juan's road to salvation, and although her own redemption seems somewhat questionable from an orthodox point of view, her faith in Don Juan and in love are, according to Tolstoy, strongly exonerating factors.

Despite its fundamental seriousness, *Don Juan* also has an admixture of humor, which is probably due less to the heritage of Da Ponte[7] than to Tolstoy's own predilection for fun. While the tendency of most Romantics was to reduce the role of Lepor-ello, thus heightening the seriousness of the play, in Tolstoy's poem Leporello is as cunning and gay as in Da Ponte, and possibly even more independent. Two scenes, especially, belong to Leporello: the first scene when he is questioned by the Holy Tribunal about Don Juan's character, and the scene in Part Two when Leporello impersonates the papal nuncio, Hieronymus. These scenes not only give an excellent characterization of Le-porello, they also make fun of the Inquisition and of the slavish obedience of man. In the scene at the Tribunal, Leporello repeats several times Don Juan's alleged words in order to vex the holy brethren:

> "Sviatye brat'ia glupy." Dazhe stydno
> Peredavat' mne vam takie rechi.
> No chasto slyshal ia, kak Don Zhuan
> Govarival: "Sviatye brat'ia glupy." . . .

"The holy brethren are stupid." I am
Quite ashamed to tell you these words.
But I heard quite often how Don Juan
Would say: "The holy brethren are stupid." . . .

When Leporello impersonates Hieronymus before the officer
who is sent to arrest Don Juan, he reads him a sermon on obedience, forgetting in his indignation that his example is not quite
in keeping with his saintly office:

Povinovenie est' to, chto esli
Ia prikazhu tebe pliasat' kachuchu,
To dolzhen ty ee pliasat', poka . . .
Poka ia ne skazhu: dovol'no! Esli zh
Ne khvatit sil tvoikh i ty umresh',
Ty dolzhem umeret', a vse pliasat'! . . .

Obedience is, if
I order you to dance the cachucha,
Then you must dance it until . . .
Until I tell you: enough! If, however,
You won't have enough strength and you die,
Then you must die and still dance . . .

Leporello finishes his sermon by giving the officer a daily pen-
ance of "one hundred and fifty genuflections, thirty Pater Nosters,
and fifty Ave Marias." It is one of the funniest scenes in the poem.

In Tolstoy's over-all work, Don Juan occupies a transitory
position between his narratives-in-verse and his tragedies. Written soon after *John Damascenus*, it shows a pronounced lyrical
strain. This is especially felt in the prologue, which is made up
of a number of lyric poems glorifying God and the beauty of
the world. Similarly, there are separate songs in the poem, such
as Don Juan's "The golden edges of distant Alpucharra are
getting dim" ("Gasnut dal'nei Al'pukharry zolotistye kraia");
"Quietly, the fragrant night" ("Mirno noch' blagovonnaia");
and the song of the monks in the epilogue, "In this terrible moment" ("V eto strashnoe mgnoven'e"). Some of the most beautiful lines of the poem are the lyric monologues of the main
characters, such as Don Juan's first monologue "Take heed, Don
Juan" ("Opomnis', Don Zhuan"), Don Octavio's declaration
of love "No, I cannot be silent before you any longer" ("Net,
ia ne mogu molchat' pred vami dole"), or Don Juan's words

to Doña Anna in her villa "The firmament is clear" ("Iasen svod nebes").

The treatment of the subject is philosophical rather than dramatic, and Tolstoy's concern is more with the exposition of his ideas than with action—which is already predictable and known. The predominance of the lyric and philosophic elements ultimately affected the fate of the poem in the theater. Despite the fact that Tolstoy considered it easily adaptable for the stage, it is better read than acted. The few attempts at staging *Don Juan* which were made at the beginning of this century proved unsuccessful.

But *Don Juan* nevertheless shares some elements with Tolstoy's later tragedies. It was the longest poetic work that Tolstoy had written up to that time. It was written predominantly in blank verse, just as were the later tragedies. In this Tolstoy was probably following the example of Pushkin's "Stone Guest," just as he followed the example of Pushkin's *Boris Godunov* in his trilogy. The language of *Don Juan* in its choice of vocabulary and in sentence structure (apart from the lyrical poems and monologues) also approaches the pattern of prose.

If *John Damascenus* may be termed Tolstoy's artistic credo, *Don Juan* is his philosophic-religious credo. And the depth of its thought and feeling makes it one of Tolstoy's most interesting and profound works.

CHAPTER 9

Dramatic Works

TOLSTOY'S tragedies are ultimately his most significant and monumental work. They consist of the trilogy, *The Death of Ivan the Terrible, Czar Fyodor, Czar Boris*, and the uncompleted tragedy, *The Governor*. Russian historical drama around the middle of the nineteenth century was unimpressive in terms of both quality and quantity. Pushkin's attempt at creating a new Shakespearian drama with his *Boris Godunov* proved unsuccessful and resulted only in a few conventionally pretty works, such as Mey's *Maid of Pskov*, or Ostrovsky's historical chronicles. Tolstoy was in general much more deeply immersed in history than these writers and was more philosophically inclined in evaluating it. History to him was both a theme as such and a pretext for speaking about universal philosophical problems. The theme of the trilogy—the tragic idea of autocracy—was simultaneously the theme of Asia versus Europe, despotism versus individual freedom. But this alone would not have made Tolstoy's tragedies what they are. They also gave the poet the possibility to manifest another aspect of his poetic talent which had been rarely evident before, namely his capacity for fine psychological characterization. This capacity finds its most perfect expression in the hero of Tolstoy's second tragedy, Czar Fyodor, who has been termed "one of the most interesting figures in Russian literature."[1] The parallels drawn between him and Dostoevsky's Prince Myshkin (*The Idiot*) testify to the complexity of his image and to an unexpected kinship between two quite dissimilar artistic natures.[2]

I *The Trilogy*

Tolstoy's interest in history, dating back to his work in the Moscow Archives in the 1830's, found its artistic expression in *Prince Serebryany* and in his "Moscow" ballads of the early 1840's.

134

Work on *Prince Serebryany* which dragged out over two decades, seems to have kept the poet's attention on that period, and as soon as he finished the novel (in 1862) he began work on *The Death of Ivan the Terrible*. The play was completed within a year (by the end of 1863), and was published in *Notes of the Fatherland* in 1866. In connection with the proposed staging of the play (the première of which took place in St. Petersburg in 1867), Tolstoy wrote a "Project for the Staging of the Tragedy *The Death of Ivan the Terrible*," which gave a detailed interpretation of the characters and the idea of the tragedy.[3]

Toward the latter part of 1864 Tolstoy went on to his next tragedy which he called *Czar Fyodor*. However, work on it did not proceed as smoothly as on the first tragedy, and it was only in 1868 that the play was completed and published in *The Messenger of Europe*. An explanatory brochure for the staging of *Czar Fyodor* was also published. But the play did not reach the stage during Tolstoy's lifetime, since it was found "unsuitable" by a special censorship commission set up for that purpose (cf. Tolstoy's life, p. 35, above; cf. the humorous epistles to Feofil Tolstoy, pp. 101-2, above). Soon after finishing *Czar Fyodor*, Tolstoy embarked on his third tragedy, entitled *Czar Boris*. He finished it about a year later in 1869, and it appeared in *The Messenger of Europe* in 1870. Although *Czar Boris* passed censorship, it was not accepted by the Imperial theaters, and the first performance of the play took place only in 1881. A general revival of Tolstoy's trilogy followed even later, with the creation of the Moscow Art Theater under the direction of Nemirovich-Danchenko and Stanislavsky at the turn of the century.

Tolstoy was not planning a trilogy when he started writing *The Death of Ivan the Terrible*. Rather, it grew out of the poet's continued preoccupation with the historical period which he had chosen, and the characters that dominated it. The contrast between Ivan the Terrible and his meek son Fyodor must have fired his imagination. Besides, he had left an "open end" in his characterization of Boris Godunov, whose development went beyond "the frame of the tragedy [*The Death of Ivan the Terrible*] forming, as it were, a prologue to a new drama."[4] Thus, despite the fact that each tragedy is a self-contained unit, together they form a whole and are connected by historical chronology, personages, and themes.

The historical background to the tragedies is the period 1584 to 1605, the final years of old Muscovite Russia prior to its collapse in the Times of Trouble (*Smutnoe vremia*). Ivan the Terrible, who had ruled Russia for over thirty years with an iron fist, died in 1584, leaving as his successor his weak, sickly son Fyodor (after having killed his abler, older son, Ivan, in a fit of rage in 1581). Since Fyodor was completely unfit to rule, government soon passed into the hands of Boris Godunov, one of Ivan's advisers, and Fyodor's brother-in-law (Fyodor was married to Godunov's sister, Irina). Despite the struggle with old boyar families who envied his position, Godunov proved to be on the whole a wise and popular ruler. His only blemish was the alleged murder of prince Dmitry—Ivan's young son by his last marriage with Maria Nagaya—in 1591, which opened the road to his own succession to the throne (Fyodor died childless, and there were no other direct heirs).[5] Upon the death of Fyodor in 1598, his wife Irina who was intelligent and well loved by the people chose to retire to a convent, and the country suddenly found itself without a ruler. A special Council (*Zemsky sobor*) then unanimously elected Boris Godunov as Czar, and the latter acceded to its request after some hesitation (interpreted by his enemies as proof of extreme slyness). Godunov's reign was encumbered by continued hostility of the boyars and by crop failure, hunger, and popular discontent. When a pretender to the throne appeared claiming that he was Dmitry, the son of Ivan the Terrible, miraculously saved from Godunov's murderous attempts, unrest in Russia came to a climax. Polish troops and discontented Cossacks joined Dmitry, while Godunov's forces, fighting without conviction, suffered defeat. At the height of disorders in 1605, Godunov died and the Pretender entered Moscow and was crowned Czar. But only a year later, dissatisfaction with the Czar's Polish, Catholic leanings led to a boyar plot, resulting in Dmitry's murder. Further unrest and struggle with the Poles and with a new "Dmitry" finally resulted in the election of Mikhail Romanov—a cousin of the deceased Czar Fyodor—Czar of all Russia in 1613.

Tolstoy's main historical source for the trilogy was Karamzin's *History of the Russian State*.[6] From it Tolstoy took not only the basic facts about the events of the period (even though he permitted himself a considerable number of historical anachronisms[7]), but also some attitudes and formal devices. Although Tolstoy disagreed with Karamzin's essentially positive attitude toward the Moscow period, he shared with him a moralistic, didactic evaluation of history; more specifically, he shared Karamzin's view of Godunov's guilt in the murder of Dmitry. Finally, Karamzin's language, the language of a writer-turned-historian had definite affinity for Tolstoy, and he relied upon him in matters of language, characterization, and atmosphere. Yet despite this strong reliance on Karamzin, Tolstoy's tragedies are not simply historical chronicles; history underwent significant reworking by Tolstoy to suit his idea of dramatic form, as well as his philosophic and artistic views.

II   The Death of Ivan the Terrible

Tolstoy's first tragedy, *The Death of Ivan the Terrible* (*Smert' Ioanna Groznogo*) is his most somber, yet dramatically most effective work. The classical unities of time, place, and action are strictly observed. The play starts in 1584 in Moscow and ends there a few months later, while all action is unified around the figure of Ivan to whose death the five acts of the drama are devoted. Yet it is not only a tragedy of external action, but also a psychological drama, a character study. Three successive phases in Ivan's psychological condition are shown in the play; at first he is dejected and desirous of leaving the world; this is followed by his "awakening to life" as a result of some favorable military news, and his wish to continue with the exercise of power; the last phase is Ivan's realization that his star is setting, and his preparation for death.

The play opens upon a stormy session of the boyar council (*duma*) which has been ordered by the Czar to elect a successor to him from amongst their midst, for in a fit of autocratic depression Ivan has decided to give up his throne. When he is first seen (Act 1, Scene 2) he appears as an inconsolable penitent who can think of nothing but his many crimes, is tired of power, and wants to retire to a monastery to expiate his sins. But three external jolts bring about a gradual transformation of his mood: the first is the arrival of a messenger from Pskov who tells of a Russian victory over the Poles; the second is an insulting letter from Prince Kurbsky (a defector to the Polish side) which

enrages Ivan, particularly since he cannot harm his enemy; the
third is the arrival of the boyar delegation. Although only a
short time ago Ivan had wished to leave the world, now the
thoughts that the boyars might have indeed carried out his orders
fills him with rage. When Godunov, the spokesman for the boyars,
tells the Czar that they want him to remain their ruler, Ivan is
stunned. But in a new shift of mood he vents his anger on them
for wanting to force him "like a prisoner" to remain on the
throne. And after a melodramatic speech in which he compares
himself to a shattered ship that has been denied haven, he finally
agrees to continue his rule.

Ivan remains in a state of consciousness of power in the following two acts. He disregards the advice of the loyal boyar
Zakharin not to divorce his wife in order to marry Lady Mary
Hastings (a relative of Queen Elizabeth of England). He shows
himself cruel and unfeeling toward his wife Maria, whom he
informs of his plans. He continues this tone of supremacy and
arrogance with Haraburda, the messenger of the Polish king
whom he mocks for serving an "elected" rather than "God-given"
ruler (Act 3). But suddenly a blow is struck against Ivan's self-
confidence: Haraburda conveys to him a challenge by the
Polish king, and tells him of a recent Russian defeat. Ivan is
overcome, then breaks out in rage, and tries to kill Haraburda
by flinging an ax at him. Despite Godunov's confirmation of the
truth of the Polish messenger's words, he refuses to believe them,
since to him they are synonymous with his own defeat. Nevertheless, this moment marks the beginning of Ivan's psychological decline, the beginning of his death, to which the last
two acts are devoted.

Just as firmly and passionately as he previously believed in
his power, Ivan now begins to believe in its termination. Military
reverses and a comet which mysteriously appears in the sky
serve to awaken Ivan's superstition, and he becomes convinced
of the imminence of his death. Still, he meets this thought with
dignity and calm: "Get up and don't snivel!" he tells his son
Fyodor who breaks out in lamentation. Ivan is willing to die,
but he wants to do it like a good Christian after having set all
his spiritual and worldly affairs in order. Despite the enormity
of his crimes, he is convinced that he can expiate them by per-
forming all necessary church rituals. His only fear is to die before

confessing, and since he suspects even his own physician and the boyars of evil designs on his immortality, he calls for two magicians. They not only confirm Ivan's presentiment, but even fix the date of his death—March 18. And it is quite in keeping with Ivan's character to put the magicians into prison after their prediction.

The final act is a masterful presentation of Ivan's psychology, on a par with the colorful first act. Ivan, who had so firmly believed in his death as to seem to wish for it, now suddenly wants to live. He is tense and nervous, for he feels that the somber prediction poisons the air. He tries to ignore it while selecting gifts for the Queen of England and for his future bride, Lady Hastings, but the boyars are silent, and so Ivan decides to prove the prediction wrong by ordering the execution of the magicians. He sends Godunov to tell them of the sentence and to see "what faces they will make." Waiting for the return of Godunov, Ivan plays chess and listens to the prattle of his jester, but his internal tension is rising. Godunov's initial ominous silence upon his return; the message of the magicians that "their science is exact" and that "the day is not over yet"; and most of all, Ivan's sudden realization that it is Godunov, his trusted servant who wants his death, combine as the final death blow against the shattered system of the Czar. Trying vainly to warn Fyodor, he staggers and falls dead on the floor, leaving everyone except Godunov in turmoil and confusion.

III *Characterization of Ivan*

The most outstanding feature of the tragedy is Tolstoy's characterization of Ivan. The poet has gone a far step beyond the essentially bloodthirsty (even if at times impressive) tyrant whom he had portrayed in *Prince Serebryany*. Tolstoy's Ivan in the tragedy resembles a complete scale of colors—from extreme dark to light, from tyranny to wisdom and humility. In his "Project for the Staging of the Tragedy *The Death of Ivan the Terrible*" Tolstoy wrote: "Ivan is not simply a villain or madman like a Nero, he has a goal, he even wants Russia's good, although, of course, in his own way ... He believes in his calling and in his infallibility in matters of government; he is convinced that even if he may err as a man, he can never err as a Czar! ... Ivan is deeply unhappy ... if he gave himself over to debauchery, debauchery did not satisfy him but only drowned for a while his internal suffering ... if he was Russia's executioner, he was also his own executioner. ... ."[8] Although the poet does not minimize Ivan's arbitrariness and unlimited self-will, he endows him with one important redeeming feature: sincerity. Ivan never acts, even though he likes melodramatic situations and speeches (cf. Act 1). He is as sincerely humble at one moment as he is proud in the next, moderate and wise now, and impulsive and extreme immediately thereafter. And behind his excesses and crimes one senses a different Ivan—a man who is intelligent, endowed with tremendous energy and will, and who could have been a great ruler. It is this Ivan who reconciles the spectator with him and makes him a truly tragic figure.

Ivan's character dominates so strongly in the tragedy that the other characters remain in the shadow. Even Godunov, Ivan's only serious antagonist, seems pale and indistinct compared to him. Possibly this was in part intended by the poet in order to make the ending more dramatic; in part, however, it seems to reflect Tolstoy's own ambiguous attitude toward the figure of Godunov whom he disliked, yet did not want to make a complete villain. Thus ambition and intrigue combine in him with sincerity and unselfishness, with the baser instincts ultimately triumphing.

The sole positive character in the play, the old boyar Zakharin —a counterpart to Morozov in *Prince Serebryany*—is only noteworthy as the spokesman for the moral idea of the play, when he utters his last words over the dead body of the Czar:

> ... O tsar' Ivan! Prosti tebia Gospod'!
> Prosti nas vsekh! Vot samovlast'ia kara!
> Vot reaspaden'ia nashego iskhod!

> ... O Czar Ivan! May the Lord forgive you!
> Forgive us all! This is the penalty for despotism!
> This is the result of our deterioration!

The same idea of guilt and retribution is expressed by the epigraph taken from the book of Daniel which tells of God's terrible punishment of king Nebuchadnezzar of Babylon. Yet this strong admixture of moral didacticism does not impair the tragedy, and fits well its tight dramatic structure and its language.

IV Dramatic Structure

As in his later tragedies, Tolstoy alternates in *The Death* between agitated mass scenes and quiet monologues, gradually building up to a climax. The noisy scene of the boyar council in Act 1, Scene 1 is contrasted to the pious, somber scene in Ivan's chamber (Scene 2); the highpoint of *The Death* occurs in Act 3 when Haraburda flings a glove at Ivan's feet as a sign of the Polish king's challenge; the final act with its retardation of the catastrophe is a masterpiece of dramatic construction.

The motif of prediction which affects not only Ivan but also Godunov (to whom the magicians predict the crown) heightens the suspense. An effective macabre note is added to it by the inopportune appearance of the buffoons at the moment of Ivan's death. Written in blank verse, in colorful Russian with an archaic flavor, the tragedy abounds in pithy statements, as in Godunov's first speech when he says: "There is great power in habit; habit for people is either a whip or a bridle" ("Velikaia v obychae est' sila; privychka liudiam—bich ili uzda"), alluding to man's desire for authority and his fear of freedom. At the height of power and pride Ivan says: "That which I don't know, that does not exist!" ("Chego zh ne znaiu ia—togo i net!"). And Godunov's faith in fate and chance is aptly expressed in such lines as "Fate does not raise us above the crowd, it only puts chance in our hands" ("Nas ne sud'ba voznosit nad tolpoiu, ona lish' sluchai v ruki nam daet"). The occasional use of Church Slavonic (in Kurbsky's letter, and in Ivan's confession to the boyars) is well integrated into the rest of the dialogue and serves to underline the importance of these passages. Tolstoy's skillful utilization of language in the trilogy belongs to one of its most outstanding features next to his characterization.

V Czar Fyodor

In contrast to *The Death of Ivan the Terrible*, a serene atmosphere characterizes *Czar Fyodor*. The oppressive, stormy rule of Ivan is giving way to a new, freer life in which various forces begin to stir. Dramatically, too, *Czar Fyodor* differs from *The Death* in being more complex and diffuse. Although the unity of place (Moscow) is preserved, the time and duration of action are only vaguely mentioned as "toward the end of the sixteenth

century." And whereas all action revolved around Ivan in the
first tragedy, here it is split up among a number of secondary
characters and situations. *Czar Fyodor* is both a character study
and a play with a definite intrigue.

The plot is concerned with the power struggle between Godunov and the Princes Shuysky who object to the former's usurp-
ation of power. Personal rivalry is enhanced by a fundamental,
theoretical conflict between the two factions, for the Shuyskys
represent old, conservative Russia while Godunov stands for a
new, more liberal (Western) orientation.[9] This conflict becomes
the moving force of the tragedy which ends with Godunov's
victory and the destruction of his enemies. A love plot between
Princess Mstislavskaya and Prince Shakhovskoy is closely connected with the power struggle, but its importance for the
tragedy is slight, for all it does is to introduce a touch of lyricism
into the play and to add a personal note to the final catastrophe.
In all this struggle Fyodor, the main character, does not take
part, but is like an axis around which everything revolves. Tolstoy
conceived of his function in the play as that of "ancient Greek
destiny, pushing its heroes forward toward the inevitable catastrophe."[10] In keeping with his passive role, Fyodor does not
change as Ivan did; he remains much the same at the end of
the tragedy as he was at its beginning.

The action in *Czar Fyodor* opens with a scene in the house of
Prince Ivan Petrovich Shuysky, where plots against the weak,
childless Czar Fyodor are being hatched. One plan calls for
Fyodor to divorce his wife Irina—thus eliminating Godunov's
influence—and to marry a princess from the Shuysky party; the
other plan is to start an open rebellion against Fyodor by pro-
claiming Dmitry (the infant son of Ivan the Terrible and his
last wife) Czar. Prince Ivan Petrovich Shuysky, an honorable
and kindly man, feels sorry for Irina and, although he hates
Godunov, signs the petition for the Czar's divorce with great
distaste—as a last resort. Godunov, in the meantime, is informed
of the boyar plot through a spy and takes his countermeasures.
Only Fyodor is ignorant of everything, even of the obvious
enmity of the Shuyskys and Godunov. When he accidentally
hears of it, he enthusiastically sets about to reconcile them, for
one of Fyodor's strongest emotions is his desire for good, for
peace and love among all men. The whole second act, one of

the most impressive and colorful ones in the tragedy, is devoted
to the meeting of the hostile parties under the aegis of Fyodor.
It masterfully shows the cunning diplomacy of Godunov, the
straightforwardness of Shuysky, Irina's "wisdom of heart," and
most of all, Fyodor's childlike guilelessness and naïveté. When
under pressure from all sides, Godunov and Shuysky give each
other their hands, Fyodor is ecstatic, and believes that everything
is well. But when Shuysky's followers, who distrust Godunov, beg
Fyodor to protect them, the latter proves completely incapable
of handling the situation. Shutting his ears with his fingers, he
leaves the scene, referring them, paradoxically, to their enemy,
Godunov: "Tell everything to Boris! Everything!" he shouts.

VI   *Characterization of Fyodor*

In *The Death of Ivan the Terrible* the dying Czar had called
Fyodor disparagingly a "bell-ringer," for Fyodor is deeply and
genuinely pious. It is significant that when he appears for the
first time on the scene he comes from a monastery where he had
admired the beauty of its bells. At the end of the tragedy Fyodor
desperately wants to retire from the world and has to be re-
minded by Irina that he cannot do so. Religious matters interest
him much more than affairs of state which he regards only as
unpleasant intrusions into his life of religious contemplation.
This comes out clearly in Act 3 when Godunov comes to him
to discuss government matters. Fyodor is vexed, tries to feign
ill health, and only most unwillingly agrees to listen to Godunov's
report. His questions show his utter ignorance of political matters, but although ignorant and naïve, Fyodor is not deceived
about his own inability to rule. Therefore, his decision to do
without Godunov rather than compromise his conscience has
special moral weight. Godunov, after exiling Shuysky's followers
—despite his assurances to the contrary—goes further and demands the arrest and execution of the Shuyskys for rebellion.
But Fyodor refuses, and accepts Godunov's resignation, humbly
admitting his own insufficiency:

> Ia ne khotel prestola. Vidno, Bogu
> Ugodno bylo, chtob nemudryi tsar'
> Sel na Rusi. Kakov ia est', takim

Ia dolzhen ostavat'sia: ia ne vrpave
Khitro vpered raschityvat', chto budet!

I did not want the throne. Apparently
It was God's will to have a simple Czar
Rule over Russia. I must remain
Such as I am; I don't have the right
To calculate cunningly, what will happen!

This moment marks the high point of Fyodor's moral character and is one of the most touching scenes in the tragedy.

But Fyodor does not remain on this high level and in the next act he is seen giving in to his weaker self. It is his intense love for Irina which makes Fyodor finally forsake his original intention of sparing the Shuyskys. When Prince Ivan Petrovich comes to him and confesses to having started a rebellion against him, Fyodor forgives him and begs him only to undo what he had started. But when the petition for his divorce falls—belatedly— into his hands, Fyodor erupts in anger and indignation. Despite Irina's pleas to wait and think, he signs the fateful order for the arrest of the Shuyskys and restores Godunov to his former power, giving him free hand to act as he pleases.

The final act brings the results of Fyodor's impulsive action. When he wants to pardon the Shuyskys he is told that Prince Ivan Petrovich "hanged himself" in prison, while Prince Shakhovskoy (the fiancé of Mstislavskaya) was shot. When he inquires about his half-brother Dmitry whom he wanted to bring to Moscow from Uglich, he is told that Dmitry died after having fallen on his knife in a fit of epilepsy. For a moment the terrible suspicion that Godunov is behind all these deaths dawns on Fyodor, but Godunov manages to dispel it and wins him again to his side. The simultaneous news of an invasion by a Tatar khan adds external danger to Fyodor's grief and diverts his attention. Left standing alone with only a few retainers at the end of the tragedy, Fyodor's words to Irina are filled with profound pathos and a sense of defeat:

Moeiu,
Moeiu vinoi sluchilos' vse! A ia—
Khotel dobra, Arina! Ia khotel
Vsekh soglasit', vse sgladit'!—Bozhe, Bozhe!
Za chto menia postavil ty tsarem!

Through my—
My own fault it all happened! And I
Wanted good, Irina! I wanted
To bring them all together, to smooth it all out!
O my God, my God! Why did you make me Czar!

With Fyodor, Tolstoy created his most controversial and most interesting character. Not only was Fyodor considered "a pamphlet against the monarchy,"[11] but also artistically a failure. Critics held that "such a weak character [was] suitable only for vaudeville"[12] and not for tragedy. Tolstoy himself, however, preferred Fyodor to Ivan and to Godunov, and retained a special affection for him. There is no doubt that he embodied in Fyodor some of his own moral and spiritual ideals. Although there is some similarity between Fyodor and Tolstoy's earlier hero, Prince Serebryany—both utterly good, noble, and incorruptible—Fyodor is much more complex and therefore more credible. Spiritual duality is his main characteristic; it is as if there were two people in him, one of whom is "weak, limited, at times even ridiculous; the other, on the contrary, is great by his humility and . . . moral loftiness."[13] The interplay of Fyodor's strength and weaknesses runs through the whole tragedy. Only once does the sublime being in him triumph over the weak (Act 3), but this triumph is short-lived. For the most part, the weak and the lofty human being are seen simultaneously. Thus, he appears for the first time in the short scene of Act 1—other-worldly, childishly naïve and rash, filled with great love for Irina, and an overwhelming desire to do good.

It is significant that all these elements contain the germ of the oncoming catastrophe: Fyodor's desire to do good triggers the whole action, while his inability to rule, his love for his wife, and his rashness result in the doom of the Shuyskys. Fyodor is a failure as a Czar; whenever he tries to act as an autocrat, he commits grievous mistakes. As a human being, however, he attains heights which are never reached by anyone around him. As in Prince Serebryany and in Dostoevsky's Prince Myshkin, there are in Fyodor traces of a *blazhenny* (a fool-in-Christ), a man who is not of this world, does not understand it, and cannot cope with it. The tragedy of Fyodor is the impotence of good in a world of intrigue and evil. After his defeat Fyodor retreats even further into religion, while Dostoevsky's Prince Myshkin escapes into madness.

VII   Characterization of Irina

Fyodor's point of view is strengthened by the presence of another character who is much like him: it is Irina, Tolstoy's most attractive heroine. Although more energetic and worldly than Fyodor, she purposefully keeps in the background in order to bolster his self-confidence. All her life is devoted to Fyodor to whom she is companion, wife, and mother. Her "wisdom of heart" is especially noticeable in the reconciliation scene between Shuysky and Godunov (Act 2) and in the confrontation between Shuysky and Fyodor (Act 4). Her strict adherence to what is right leads her to oppose her brother's methods and to a growing estrangement between them which culminates in the third tragedy.

VIII   Characterization of Godunov

Godunov assumes, of course, a much more important role in *Czar Fyodor* than he had in *The Death,* for he and Shuysky are the principal "active" actors in the drama. As the real force behind the weak and irresolute Fyodor, Godunov must not only govern, but also fight continuously for his position which is threatened on all sides. He manages to forestall the movements of his enemies by keeping a step ahead of them through cunning calculation, bribery, and threats. Yet the villain in Godunov is only one aspect of his character; the other is that of a statesman, conscious of his power and proud of his accomplishments, as when he enumerates to Shuysky Russia's achievements: peace with Lithuania, Germany, Sweden, and Denmark; an advantageous treaty with England; defeat of the Tatar khan and others (Act 2). The elimination of the Shuyskys is desired by Godunov for political rather than personal reasons, for they are interfering with his plans for a new Russia by obstinately clinging to the old. In Act 5, Godunov confides to Irina his dream—to build a powerful state, a "new, prudent Russia." This patriotic note contributes to Godunov's greater appeal in this part of the trilogy.

The touchstone of Godunov's character—from a moral point of view—is the question of his guilt in the murder of Dmitry, and although it is obvious that Godunov is responsible for the crime, Tolstoy introduces an element of fate as a mitigating factor. In light of this, Godunov's responsibility for Dmitry's death assumes the nature of a fateful concurrence of events which force Godunov to act as he does. He does not want Dmitry's murder; his monologue in Act 4 ("I have been suspended! Fyodor himself seems to force me" / "Ia otreshen! Sam Fedor slovno nudit!"/) shows him at crossroads, and his internal flight is further illustrated in his dialogue with Kleshnin, Fyodor's attendant, in which Godunov never actually gives an order for Dmitry's murder. Thus, gradually and somewhat unexpectedly for the author himself, the figure of Godunov grew in stature, complexity, and tragic dimension in the course of the second tragedy.

Although *Czar Fyodor* is written in blank verse like *The Death,* there are some prose passages in it—dialogues of the people in Acts 4 and 5—which are suggestive of the example of Pushkin's *Boris Godunov* (cf. below). Another feature which distinguishes the tragedy from *The Death* is the abundance of monologues by the main characters, providing them with the opportunity to explain themselves through words rather than action. Such are Shuysky's monologue in Act 1 in which he tries to find a justification for his rebellion against Fyodor ("My path is not straight"/ "Moi put' ne priam"/); Godunov's monologue in Act 2, a defense of his policies before Shuysky: ("When the country, after long disorders"/"Kogda zemlia po dolgom neustroistve"); Fyodor's touching declaration of independence in Act 3: "Yes, brother-in-law, yes" ("Da, shurin, da"); and finally, Godunov's splendid monologue in Act 5 in which he takes stock of the past and speaks of his dream of a new Russia: "Czar Ivan was/ like/ a high mountain" ("Vysokaia gora byl tsar' Ivan"). Even though the dramatic tension is somewhat weakened by this device, it is compensated by a number of impressive scenes, such as the reconciliation scene in Act 2, the dramatic encounter between Fyodor, Shuysky, and Godunov in Act 3 (the high point of the play), and the quick succession of disasters in Act 5. In terms of characterization and tragic impact *Czar Fyodor* is undoubtedly Tolstoy's most interesting and profound work.

IX   Czar Boris

Czar Boris, the final part of the trilogy, is again somber and
dark. Tolstoy seems to have combined various elements from
the two earlier tragedies in it. *Czar Boris* is, like *The Death*, a
character study of its hero, and concentrates on the portrayal
of his death. Like Ivan, Godunov is seen in three stages of his
psychic condition: at first in full glory and in the firm belief
that the end justifies the means; then, in the face of calamity
he is forced to fight against his domestic and foreign enemies;
finally, realizing that he is doomed, he accepts his fate and dies.
A diffuse dramatic structure, a subplot (involving Godunov's
daughter Ksenia and her Danish fiancé, Khristian), and a large
number of characters, on the other hand, are reminiscent of
Czar Fyodor.

The action of *Czar Boris* is vaguely dated as about seven years
after the events in *Czar Fyodor*.[14] Godunov has finally reached
his goal and has become Czar of Russia. The procession of
numerous ambassadors whom he receives after his coronation
serves to underline the brilliancy of his position, and forms a
striking contrast to the ending of the tragedy. Filled with happiness, Godunov wants not only his own family, but the whole
nation to participate in the festivities, and invites the people to
his palace. In the first monologue at the end of the act, he takes
stock of his actions, justifies them, and consciously underlines
the break with the past:

> Razorvana otnyne
> S proshedshim sviaz'! Perezhita pora
> Kromeshnoi t'my—siiaet solntse snova—
> I derzhit skiptr dlia pravdy i dobra
> Lish' tsar' Boris—net bole Godunova!

> With the past is severed! The time of
> From now on the connection
> Complete darkness has been overcome—the sun shines again—
> And it is Czar Boris who holds the scepter
> For truth and goodness—There is no Godunov any more!

He persists in his attitude of happiness even after his encounter
with his sister Irina, who, having become a nun after Fyodor's
death, condemns him and tells him never to forget his guilt

and to expiate it by good deeds. "Time will show which one of us is right," Boris tells her on leaving. But a blow is struck against him soon (Act 2) when rumors of Dmitry being alive reach him. Boris knows that Dmitry is dead, yet he cannot name his proofs without incriminating himself, and must be silent even in his own family. He realizes that his enemies, the Romanovs (distant relatives of Ivan the Terrible) are waiting for a chance to ruin him. But Czar Boris does not want to use reprisals, and it is ironical that it is now his brother, Semyon Godunov, who demands that the Romanovs be delivered into his hands, just as Godunov had demanded the delivery of the Shuyskys from Fyodor in the earlier tragedy.

In Acts 3 and 4 Boris begins to fight against the various enemies that threaten his throne. At first he tries means of persuasion: Vasily Shuysky, a nephew of Prince Ivan Petrovich, is asked to testify before the people about Dmitry's death which he investigated on Godunov's orders. Dmitry's mother, Maria Nagaya, is brought to the capital to testify, but both these means fail. Finally, when disorders begin to grow and Godunov's armies are defeated by those of the false Dmitry, Boris resorts to measures of terror which he had hoped to forego. The death of Khristian (who is poisoned by the "Russian" party at the court) adds personal sorrow to the heavy burden of the czar.

Act 5 brings on the catastrophe. In a nightmarish vision Dmitry's ghost appears to Boris in the throne hall and shatters his nerves. A confrontation with Kleshnin (who gave the order for Dmitry's murder and who has since become a monk) brings no solace either. Boris realizes that in his fight with the specter of his guilt he has been defeated and that his end is near. In a final effort to consolidate the throne, he collects the boyars and asks them to swear fidelity to his son Fyodor. During the banquet Boris feels faint and dies in the midst of his grieving family and gloating boyars. The curtain falls on a scene that implies the beginning of even greater unrest and trouble.

X *Characterization of Boris*

Tolstoy's conception of Boris underwent considerable change, in a positive direction, in the course of the trilogy. In *Czar Fyodor* the wise statesman began to outweigh the cold intriguer of *The Death*. *Czar Boris* became a final glorification of Godunov, a kind of pedestal especially erected for him. Boris assumes many new, likeable features in the final part of the trilogy. Personal ambition no longer dominates him, having given way to profound devotion to Russia and its welfare. In his conversations with the foreign ambassadors in Act 1 Boris shows justice, diplomatic skill, and dignity. He has become an ideal, popular Czar who is accessible to everyone, and who orders the doors of the palace to be opened for "between the Russian people and their Czar there are no barriers" (Act 1). As a father, he is tender and understanding and permits his children a freedom that is in strict opposition to old custom. Yet, all these ideal features make Boris less credible as a character. He is Tolstoy's "brain child," who reflects too obviously the poet's own ideas. This is especially evident in Boris' "anti-Tatar" and pro-Western attitude, when he says in Act 1:

> No v dvesti let nas igo
> Tatarskoe ot prochikh khristian
> Otrezalo. Razorvannuiu tsep'
> Ia s zapadom sviazat' nameren snova . . .

> But two hundred years of
> Tatar yoke have cut us off from
> Other Christians. I intend to resume
> The broken ties with the West . . .

He even dreams, in a strangely contemporary-sounding phrase, to overtake the West eventually in achievements. The intended marriage of his daughter Ksenia to a Danish prince is also part of Boris' Westernizing plans.

Boris' only tragic flaw is his guilt, of which the poet cannot absolve him despite his sympathies for him. On the day of his coronation Boris visits Irina in the convent:

> Esli,
> Chtob t'my liudei schastlivymi sodelat',
> Ia bol'shuiu nepravost' sovershil,
> Chem tot, kotoryi blaga nikakogo
> Im ne prines—kto zh, on il' ia, vinovnei
> Pred Gospodom?

> If
> In order to make masses of people happy,

> I committed a greater wrong
> Than he who had done no good
> To them,—who then, he or I
> Is more guilty before the Lord?

He raises the problem into an abstract, philosophical realm. But Irina, despite love and pity for her brother, cannot acquit him:

> Vse tu zhe ne tebe
> Ia vizhu ten'. Kuda by ni poshel ty,
> Vezde, vsegda, zloveshchaia, ona
> Idet s toboi. Ne vlastny my uiti
> Ot proshlogo, Boris!

> I still see the same
> Shadow upon you. No matter where you go,
> Everywhere, always, sinister, it
> Follows you. We cannot leave
> Our past, Boris!

This is finally realized by Boris himself in the last moments of his life when the whole edifice of power which he had built begins to crumble:

> Ot zla lish' zlo roditsia—vse edino:
> Sebe l' my im sluzhit' khotim il' tsarstvu—
> Ono ni nam, ni tsarstvu vprok neidet!

> From evil only evil is born—it does not matter
> Whether we want it to serve us or the land—
> Nothing good will come of it either for us,
> Or for the country!

The moral element which had been prominent in the first tragedy recurs as a concluding note in the last.

Boris dominates the tragedy as much as did Ivan in *The Death*, and therefore most of the secondary characters are unimportant.

Nevertheless, one secondary character who had occurred in the first tragedy must be mentioned. It is Maria Godunova, Boris' wife, who appears in Acts 2 and 3. Somewhat unexpectedly, Maria Godunova takes over some of Boris' earlier sinister features in this part of the trilogy. She becomes a kind of a Russian Lady Macbeth who speaks like a Russian peasant woman, and hides behind a mask of simplicity and humility. She does not openly oppose Godunov, for instance, in his plans to marry Ksenia to Khristian, yet she does everything to undermine them and finally resorts to poison. Her conversation with Godunov, filled with hidden irony and apparent humility belongs to some of the liveliest dialogues in the whole tragedy. It is also she, rather than Boris, who extracts from Dmitry's mother the admission that Dmitry is dead. Although her image is sketchy, it indicates an interesting development in Tolstoy's characterizations.

XI *Dramatic Structure*

The dramatic structure of *Czar Boris* resembles that of the earlier tragedies, although the overabundance of characters and the predominance of conversation over action somewhat impairs its impact. There is again an alternation of mass scenes with quiet monologues or dialogues. Thus, the reception of the ambassadors in Scene 1 of Act 1—probably the most splendid act in the trilogy—is contrasted to the quiet scene in the nunnery where Godunov and Irina meet (Scene 2). The lyric note of the beginning of Act 2 (the conversation between Ksenia, Khristian, and Fyodor) is contrasted with Godunov's reception of the news of Dmitry, Maria Godunova's plotting against Khristian, and the boisterous scene among the robbers in the woods, in which Tolstoy reintroduces Mit'ka, an old character from *Prince Serebryany*. The dramatic highpoint of the tragedy is built up gradually through Acts 3 and 4, and reaches its culmination in Act 5 in a series of effective scenes: Boris' vision of Dmitry's ghost; his encounter with his son Fyodor in which he is virtually forced to tell him of his guilt; and his sudden death at the banquet in honor of Basmanov. The motif of prediction recurs with added force. In Act 3 Boris recalls the prediction of the magicians in *The Death*, namely that his most dangerous enemy would be "killed but be alive"; "Killed but alive! The prediction has come true!" ("Ubit no zhiv! Sverhilos' predskazan'e!"). At the beginning of Act 5, in the nightmare scene, he repeats the same words: "Killed, but alive!"

Monologues play an important part in the structure of the tragedy, as they did in *Czar Fyodor*, and some of them belong

to the best Tolstoy had written, for example, Boris' first monologue at the beginning of Act 1: "It has happened! I wear the
crown and the imperial jewels!" ("Svershilos'! V ventse i bar-
makh ia!"). Of importance, too are Khristian's story about his
childhood and life at the beginning of Act 2, Maria Nagaya's
monologue in Act 4: "Fourteen long years have passed" ("Chety-
rnadstat' minulo dolgikh let"), and some of Boris' other monologues, mentioned above. In terms of its poetic language, rich
settings, and drama *Boris Godunov* forms a splendid conclusion
of the trilogy.

XII *Influences of Shakespeare, Schiller, and Pushkin*

In his "Project for the Staging of *Czar Fyodor*" Tolstoy stated
that his tragedies were following the laws of European drama,
primarily those of "the Germanic school which occupies itself
with the analysis and development of character" in contrast to
"the Romance school which concentrates on the intrigue." Among
specific influences, Shakespeare's "royal" tragedies, Schiller's
historical dramas, and Pushkin's *Boris Godunov* must be mentioned. The influence of Shakespeare on virtually all European
dramatists hardly needs special mention. In Russia, interest in
Shakspeare went back to the eighteenth century, when Karamzin
first translated *Julius Caesar* and wrote his commentaries on
the English dramatist (1777). The next important step in Russian Romantic (Shakespearian) drama is connected with Pushkin's *Boris Godunov*. The separation of these two influences in
Tolstoy's work is at times somewhat difficult.

Tolstoy knew Shakespeare well, although he was far from
being an uncritical admirer of the English playwright. Still, he
found parallels between his own conception of tragedy and that
of Shakespeare: "The subject of a tragedy *should be an important event, in the course of which interesting characters appear and manifest themselves.* This formula would fit equally
well *Hamlet, Coriolanus, Julius Caesar,* and *Romeo,* as it would
fit *Macbeth, King Lear,* and *Othello,* otherwise the three latter
works could not be termed tragedies at all."[15] More specifically,
Tolstoy seems to have borrowed from *Macbeth* in his early characterization of Godunov, while Maria Godunova in the last
part of the trilogy came to resemble Lady Macbeth. The influ-

ence of prediction on Godunov's action, the vision of Dmitry's ghost in the last tragedy are also suggestive of *Macbeth*. Fyodor has been compared to Hamlet, while a parallel has been drawn between Ivan and Richard III,[16] although these comparisons seem somewhat far-fetched.

More important than Shakespeare seems to have been the example of Schiller's subtle psychological characterization and his concept of tragedy in which "character and circumstances have an equal share."[17] Schiller's *Wallenstein* (1799) trilogy is mentioned time and again in Tolstoy's letters during the period he was working on his tragedies, and Wallenstein's fate and character seem to have left some imprints on Tolstoy's heroes. Wallenstein's fate is in part determined by his peculiar psychological makeup (belief in astrology and in his ability to judge human nature), and by external circumstances (pressure of his advisors, the treason of the elder Piccolomini). The same elements of character and fate determine the death of Ivan, Fyodor's tragic defeat, and Godunov's rise and fall. Moreover, Wallenstein shares with Ivan (and Godunov) belief in omens, and with Godunov a strong and fervent patriotism, which leads him to treason (as it leads Godunov to crime).

Lastly, but no less important, Pushkin's *Boris Godunov* affected Tolstoy, especially *Czar Boris*. Tolstoy's use of blank verse alternating with prose passages is derived from Pushkin. Several scenes in Tolstoy's *Czar Boris* have close counterparts in Pushkin's drama.[18] Both poets accepted the idea of Godunov's guilt in the murder of Dmitry, although their respective characterizations of Godunov were different, Pushkin being more objective and historical, and Tolstoy being more personal and philosophical.

On the historical level Tolstoy's dramas present a dark page of Russian history, determined by specific historical circumstances and personalities, and resulting in the tragedy of autocracy. In Tolstoy's interpretation they furthermore represent opposing government traditions—Oriental despotism versus European individualism—as exemplified in Ivan and in Godunov of the last tragedy.

On a more abstract, philosophical level the tragedies touch on such questions as the fickleness and ingratitude of the masses, as well as man's herd instinct and fear of independence. The most important problem in the trilogy, however, is a moral one: the question of whether a "useful" crime can be justified in view of the obvious impotence of good—a question also poignantly posed in Dostoevsky's *Crime and Punishment.* And Tolstoy's answer to this question is the same as Dostoevsky's—a clear condemnation of evil and a reaffirmation of good.

XIII The Governor (Posadnik)

In his last tragedy Tolstoy turned away from the Moscow period to early medieval Russia—his favorite epoch. The action of *The Governor* takes place in thirteenth-century Novgorod;[19] yet history per se is less important here than it had been in the trilogy, for the tragedy is moral and psychological, and its theme is the fate of "an honest man who takes upon himself an apparent villainy."[20] Tolstoy found this type of drama easier to write, since it permitted him greater liberty in the handling of the material.

Tolstoy first mentioned the idea for *The Governor* in a letter of June, 1870; by September he completed parts of the first two acts and read them to some of his friends. But then the poet lost interest in the play—Sofya Andreevna's disapproval had a definite part in it—and it was only in the following year that he began to rewrite it in verse (the first version had been in prose). However, Tolstoy's illness which was progressing rapidly, prevented him from completing the drama and the extant three acts give only a general idea of it.

The action of the play revolves around the person of the governor (*posadnik*) of Novgorod, Gleb Mironych, during the siege of the city by the princes of Suzdal who claim it as their patrimony. Two parties have formed within the beleaguered city: one, headed by the military commander (*voevoda*) Foma Grigorich, wants peace at any price; the other, headed by the governor, prefers death to defeat. The governor believes in the possibility of victory and manages to get the *veche* (popular assembly) to depose the inefficient military commander, and appoint the young and brave boyar Chermny. But Chermny comes under suspicion of treason when a party of the enemy enters the city through a secret passageway to which he alone has the key. In order to save him and his military command, the gover-

nor takes the guilt upon himself. He is judged by the *veche*
and condemned to loss of position and exile. The last two acts
which remained unwritten, were to demonstrate the governor's
innocence and to show his rehabilitation before the people of
Novgorod prior to a dramatic death.

The main action is connected with two love intrigues. One
concerns Chermny and his mistress, Natalya, who betrays him
by giving the key to the secret passageway to her brother, a
fighter on the enemy side. The other involves Vera, the governor's daughter, who is engaged to Vasilko, but refuses to marry
him before her father's name is cleared. It is she who uncovers
Natalya's guilt and makes her confess it before the people of
Novgorod, thus proving the governor's innocence.

As can be seen from the above outline, Tolstoy combined a
complicated intrigue with a character study, as he did in *Czar
Fyodor*. Indeed, the intrigue seems to dominate over characterization, which is unusual in Tolstoy. Yet its development seems
labored and not quite convincing at times. The conflict of the
two parties—the governor's and the former military commander's
—is not used to create the actual dramatic conflict, as had been
the case in *Czar Fyodor*. Rather, Tolstoy introduces a somewhat
conventional ingredient of melodrama—a secret passageway—
and ties the dramatic knot around it. The chain of events which
leads to Chermny's accusation is quite strained: when Chermny
mentions the secret passageway to the governor in a street tête-
à-tête, his mistress Natalya happens to be near and overhears
it. The only fugitive prisoner from Suzdal happens to be Natalya's
brother and happens to come to Chermny's house where Natalya
lives, although she has long been given up as dead by her kin.
Natalya's sudden recognition of his disguise and her conflict
of loyalties also has strong melodramatic overtones and belongs
to the weakest scenes in the play.

XIV *Characterization*

Characterization in *The Governor* is primarily devoted to its
hero, Gleb Mironych, who is another version of Tolstoy's ideal
characters, such as Zakharin in *The Death* and Prince Shuysky
in *Czar Fyodor*. He is uncompromisingly honest, stern, and im-
personally patriotic. Thus, in choosing Chermny as military

commander, he is not guided by personal feelings, but by his conviction that he alone can save the city. The same motif moves the governor in defending Chermny against the accusation of treason. He feels that if Chermny falls, the city will fall too, and so he sacrifices himself to prevent this. Having deposed the former military commander, Foma, the governor does not try to pacify him or win him to his side. And even when he is already losing his power, after having admitted treason, the governor refuses to accept help from him (for Foma wants to ruin Chermny rather than the governor) saying that he would "rather accept help from the devil." Many of his speeches contain moralizing sentences: "If you are afraid of gossip, you won't be able to make a step" ("Boiatsia tolkov—shagu ne stupit'"); "Be pure before yourself, not before the people" ("Ne pred liud'mi—pered soboi bud' chist!"). Although his extreme moral purity makes his fall quite spectacular, it reduces his human appeal and credibility. Furthermore, like Godunov in the last part of the trilogy, the governor becomes a spokesman for the poet's ideas, as when he elaborates his concept of real freedom:

> To keep to one's rights,
> To honor those of others, to keep law and truth.
> Not to comply with the whims of princes,
> But to do without a murmur and faithfully
> That which our lord Novgorod demands—
> This is freedom! But that everyone
> Were to be free to do what comes to his head—
> Indeed not, this would not be freedom
> But anarchy!

> Prav svoikh derzhat'sia
> Chuzhie chtit', bliusti zakon i pravdu,
> Ne prikhoti kniazhie ispolniat'
> No to chinit' bezropotno i sviato,
> Chto gosudar' nash Novgorod velit—
> Vot volia v chem! A chtoby vsiaki delat'
> Volën byl to, chto v golovu vzbredet—
> Net, to byla b ne volya—neuriad'e
> To bylo by!

Although such ideas are valid and interesting in themselves, they become too obvious in a character who has not yet been completely developed by the author.

Tolstoy planned to have four principal characters in the play, of which two were to be masculine and two feminine. To the former belonged the governor and Chermny, to the latter Vera, and either Natalya or the widow of the previous governor, Mamelfa Dmitrevna. Chermny has a subordinate role in the play, being a modified version of the governor. Like Gleb Mironych he is honest and able, although he has a weakness for women and is less stern. As a character he has no real life of his own and represents only an extension of the governor's fate. Vera, the governor's daughter, was to have a "slightly heroic role," according to Tolstoy's plan, but since Tolstoy did not finish the play, the heroic aspect remained undeveloped. Only two other feminine characters, Mamelfa Dmitrevna and Natalya, are of some interest.

In Mamelfa Dmitrevna, Tolstoy created his only feminine character role, and despite the relative brevity of her appearance, she is one of the most colorful and convincing figures in the tragedy. In her brightly delineated character she resembles Maria Godunova in the last part of the trilogy, although she lacks the latter's wickedness. Mamelfa Dmitrevna, widow of the former governor, is extremely proud, and has developed into a petty tyrant (*samodur*), used to being obeyed and feared by everyone, and delighting in her power. She does have one redeeming quality—she is honest and despises trickery and injustice, but she is easily deceived by the governor's enemies and misjudges Gleb Mironych and Chermny. She appears on the scene only once (Act 2), when she is seen visiting the governor's wife, yet her personality and manner are brought out to perfection. Being used to dominate and "to instruct," she subjects everyone in the governor's house to censure, starting with the governor's wife and daughter, and ending with Gleb Mironych himself. The latter is not to be intimidated by anyone, and although he at first listens respectfully to her, he finally loses patience and tells her to mind her own business. Mamelfa Dmitrevna makes a magnificent exit after expressing her extreme disapproval of the governor's insolence:

> Drugim davat' uroki
> A ne sebe ikh slyshat' ot drugikh
> Privykla ia. Uchit'sia blagochest'iu

I vezhestvu sbiraetsia ko mne
Ves' Novgorod. Samoi zhe nauchat'sia
Kak mne vestis'—na eto ia stara . . .

I am used to giving lessons to others
And not to hear them from anyone.
All Novgorod comes to me to learn piety
And politeness. To learn how to conduct myself—
For that I am too old . . .

Natalya is not as bright a character as Mamelfa Dmitrevna, and her role is rather small in the tragedy despite the fact that she is the cause of the governor's fall. What is interesting is her characterization suggestive of Dostoevsky's "humiliated and insulted" characters. Living with Chermny as his mistress, she is deeply conscious of her sinfulness and tries to redeem it by piety and humility. All the jewels which Chermny gives her, she presents to the church where she prays constantly for the forgiveness of her sins. She is full of humility toward her servants whom she considers morally superior. Toward Chermny she is filled with self-effacing love. The planned public confession of guilt by Natalya before the people of Novgorod also fits her Dostoevskyan nature well.

XV *Dramatic Structure*

The generally weak plot and unsatisfactory characterization are partly compensated by an effective dramatic exposition, swiftness of action, and simple language. The play starts *in medias res* with a dramatic mass scene giving the background of the tragedy and poignant characteristics of the three main protagonists: the stern governor, Chermny, and Foma. The following scene in which the governor and Chermny appear, starts the dramatic development. The second act brings on the appearance of Raguylo, Natalya's brother, and Natalya's betrayal of her lover. The third act introduces the dramatic high point: enemy forces invade the city, Chermny discovers the loss of the key, and the opposition prepares to depose him. But the governor intervenes, accuses himself, and is judged by the *veche* in another tempestuous mass scene.

Since Tolstoy had written the first version in prose, there is a much greater number of prose passages in the play than had been in the trilogy; again, most of them are used in portraying popular speech in mass scenes. The blank verse of the rest of the drama is as vivid and colorful as it had been in the earlier tragedies. Tolstoy was very careful in using colorful local terms, and in preserving the general aura of medieval Russian.

It is difficult to evaluate a tragedy on the strength of only three acts. Some critics claimed that *The Governor* would have been one of Tolstoy's best tragedies. It does possess good dramatic composition, vividness, and color. However, the poet seems to have been unable to integrate his moral ideas into the tragedy in a convincing manner, and they stick out and overshadow the rest of it. Despite some merit, *The Governor* as a whole does not reach the level of the trilogy.

CHAPTER 10

Summation

IT has been previously suggested that Tolstoy's over-all production, despite the variety of his genres, has a basic unity. Certain elements are characteristic of Tolstoy, certain themes recur in most of his works whether it be prose, poetry, or drama. A strong lyrical strain is typical for the early period, and is most strikingly manifested in his lyric poems, and in such early narratives-in-verse as *John Damascenus*. Romantic, fantastic themes are his favorites at this time, such as the intrusion of the supernatural into the world of reality in "The Vampire," some other early stories and ballads, and even in the late narratives in verse *The Portrait* and *The Dragon*. The later period is characterized by a shift to drama which is largely combined with historical themes (cf. the trilogy and the incompleted drama *The Governor*). A dramatic "trend" also finds its expression in Tolstoy's 'Moscow" ballads, in his novel *Prince Serebryany,* and in the poem *Don Juan*. History as such remains Tolstoy's favorite theme in his late ballads (cf. "The Song about Vladimir's Campaign against Chersones").

Tolstoy's literary fate is illustrative of the power of certain predominant "currents," proclaimed largely by vocal literary critics. The 1850's, 1860's, and even the 1870's had been declared a period of "Realistic" prose, so Tolstoy's "Romantic" poetry was considered to be hopelessly out of tune with the times. Tolstoy was acutely aware of his isolation and suffered keenly from the hostility of literary critics which most of his works met. The popularity which some of his poems (not always his best), his novel, and his tragedies (especially *The Death of Ivan the Terrible*) enjoyed with the public was only a partial consolation. Still, it probably kept him from stopping to write altogether. But full recognition came only posthumously with the revival of "pure" poetry by the Symbolists who saw in him a precursor, both

161

in terms of poetic themes as well as form. Today A. K. Tolstoy's position as an outstanding lyric poet is unchallenged in Russian literature, comparable to that of Nikolaus Lenau in German literature or Alfred Lord Tennyson in English literature.

Notes and References

Chapter One

1. For a detailed genealogy of the Tolstoys, see: P. I. Biriukov, *Biografiia L'va Nikolaevicha Tolstogo*, Gosizdat, Moscow-Petrograd, 1923, vol. 1, p. 4.

2. E. F. Iunge, "Vospominaniia," *Vestnik Evropy*, 1905, vol. 2, p. 801.

3. A. Lirondelle, *Le Poète Alexis Tolstoi, L'homme et l'oeuvre*. Thèse pour le doctorat es lettres, Paris, 1912, p. 5.

4. Anna Alexeevna had been on friendly terms with the family of Konstantin Petrovich's brother, Fyodor Petrovich Tolstoy, a well-known sculptor and engraver.

5. P. P. Gnedich, *Vospominaniia*, Moscow, 1929, p. 191.

6. A. Lirondelle, *op. cit.*, and A. A. Kondrat'ev, *Graf A. K. Tolstoi*, St. Petersburg, 1912, pp. 3-86.

7. It has been suggested that Perovsky may have been personally acquainted with E. T. A. Hoffmann who was residing at Dresden at that time. Cf. A. Kirpichnikov, *Ocherki po istorii novoi russkoi literatury*, "Antonii Pogorel'skii," St. Petersburg, 1896, pp. 76-120.

8. Letter to A. I. Turgenev, February 6, 1833, in *Ostaf'evskii arkhiv kniazei Viazemskikh*, vol. 3, pp. 220-21.

9. Letter to S. A. Miller, August 22, 1851.

10. Letter to A. Gubernatis, March 4, 1874.

11. A. O. Smirnova, quoted in Lirondelle, pp. 15-16.

12. Letter to S. A. Miller, July 31, 1853.

13. *Ibid.*

14. A. V. Meshcherskii, "Iz moei stariny," Vospominaniia, *Russkii Arkhiv*, 1900, No. 7, p. 3731.

15. V. D. Davydov, "Vospominaniia," *Russkii Arkhiv*, 1879, II, p. 331.

16. Lirondelle, p. 35.

17. D. I. Chizhevskii, *Gegel' v Rossii*, Paris 1939, pp. 32, 33.

18. Lev Tolstoi, quoted in *ibid.*, p. 218.

19. I. I. Zamotin, *Sorokovye i shestidesiatye gody. Ocherki po istorii russkoi literatury 19. stoletiia*, Petrograd, 1915, p. 50.

20. Letter to Ia. K. Grot, in *Perepiska Ia. K. Grota s P. A. Pletnevym*, St. Petersburg, 1896, I, p. 213.

21. Letter of May 11, 1841.

22. Derived from Tolstoy's estate Krasny Rog, just as Perovsky's pseudonym had been derived from his estate Pogoreltsy.

23. Lirondelle, p. 40.

24. Letter of February 10, 1880, published in *Vestnik Evropy*, January and February, 1908.

25. Letter to S. A. Miller, October 14, 1851; italics in the original.

26. They were actually distantly related, and there were neither close personal nor literary ties between them. Only during the winter of 1856/57 did they occasionally meet in St. Petersburg, but later drifted apart.

27. Letter to S. A. Miller, January 8, 1855.

28. Letter of October 25, 1856.

29. Letter to Alexander II, August or September, 1861.

30. *Pri dvore dvukh imperatorov*, Leningrad, 1928-29, p. 79.

31. Letter of October 25, 1856.

32. Letter of October 9, 1856.

33. Letter of February 7, 1869; italics in the original.

34. Letter to Stasiulevich, November 12, 1869.

35. N. Denisiuk, *Kriticheskaia literatura o proizvedeniiakh grafa A. K. Tolstogo*, Moscow, 1907, p. 41.

36. Letter to Markevich, January 11, 1870.

37. Letter to Sof'ia Andreevna, October 25, 1853.

38. Letter of July 20, 1871.

39. Letter of February 4, 1859; italics in the original.

40. Letter of March 21, 1861; italics in the original.

41. Letter to S. A. Miller, July 27, 1861.

42. Letter to the editor of *Russkii Vestnik*, 1862, No. 7, pp. 213-18.

43. Lirondelle, pp. 214-15.

44. Letter of July 24, 1864.

45. Carolina Sayn-Wittgenstein (1819-87) met Franz Liszt in Kiev in 1847; she left her husband a year later and became Liszt's mistress. Liszt became interested in Tolstoy's poetry, and put several of his poems to music.

46. Letter to Princess Sayn-Wittgenstein, February 20, 1867.

47. Letter of December 13, 1868.

48. Letter to Sof'ia Andreevna, August 10, 1869.

49. Letter of May 9, 1871.

50. Letter of July 25, 1871.

51. D. N. Tsertelev (1852-1911), a poet and philosopher, wrote several articles on Tolstoy's work at the beginning of the twentieth century.

52. Letter of June 19, 1875.

53. Letter of July 2, 1875.

Chapter Two

1. V. Belinskii, *Sochineniia*, M, 1895, vol. 5, pp. 359-61.
2. Preface to "The Vampire," St. Petersburg, 1899.
3. Cf. chapter on ballads, p. 81.
4. The vampire theme, cf. Goethe, "Die Braut von Korinth"; Nodier, "Smarra ou les demons de la nuit"; Merimée, "La Guzla"; the theme of a hereditary curse, cf. Tieck, *Karl von Berneck;* Grillparzer, *Die Ahnfrau;* E. T. A. Hoffmann, "Die Elexiere des Teufels"; the motif of a portrait, cf. Maturin, *Melmoth the Wanderer;* Gogol, "Portret," etc.
5. Preface to "The Vampire," St. Petersburg, 1899.
6. His mistress and companion in crime had, among other things, murdered her husband, cf. the curse in "The Vampire."
7. Lirondelle points out some parallels between Tolstoy's story and Merimée's "La Guzla" and "Constantin Yacoubovitch," cf. Lirondelle, p. 41; cf. also Pushkin's "Pesni zapadnykh slavian."
8. Cf. notes in the 1963 Soviet edition of A. K. Tolstoy, vol. 3, p. 567.
9. Letter of March 21, 1861.
10. Reworkings for the stage by G. T. Nimand (1863), S. Dobrov (1866), K. S. Barantsevich (1873), N. Semiakina (1883), and Ia. I. Iankevich (1888); reworking as opera by F. B. Gravert (during Tolstoy's lifetime), M. I. Markov (1884), G. A. Kazachenko (1888), and P. N. Triodin (1923).
11. Cf. N. Ul'ianov, *Diptikh*, New York, 1967, p. 13.
12. Letter of December 13, 1856.
13. Letter to Markevich, March 20, 1860.
14. "Byt russkogo naroda," "Pesni russkogo naroda," "Skazaniia russkogo naroda," "Russkie narodnye skazki."
15. Letter by Count V. Sollogub, February 16, 1862, published in *Vestnik Evropy*, 1895, vol. 5, p. 445.

Chapter Three

1. D. S. Mirsky, *A History of Russian Literature*, N. Y., 1958, p. 221.
2. A. K. Tolstoi, *Sobranie sochinenii*, 4 vols. Moscow, 1963, vol. 1, p. 26.
3. Emanuel Swedenborg, 1688-1772, Swedish theologian, scientist, and philosopher with a strong mystic trend. After his death his followers formed the New Church or New Jerusalem Church.
4. I. Iampol'skii, introduction to A. K. Tolstoi, *Stikhotvoreniia*, Biblioteka poeta, Leningrad, 1936, p. 54.

5. "Derevtso moe," "Kak zdes' khorosho," "Voidem siuda," and "Rastianulsia na prostore."

6. In a letter to Princess Sayn-Wittgenstein (February 5, 1875) the poet said that he had written it in a state of semiconsciousness.

Chapter Four

1. *Byliny*. Epic poems of the Russian people. A number of specific heroes reappear throughout them. The byliny are divided into cycles, such as the Kiev, Novgorod cycles. They range in time from the earliest pre-Christian period to the eighteenth century.

2. This poem, in its turn, was a translation of a German poem by I. Zedlitz.

3. Letter to Stasiulevich, January 7, 1868.

4. Letter to Markevich, February 7, 1869.

5. Cf. letter to Stasiulevich, March 10, 1869; the ballad may have been influenced by Heine's poem "Das Schlachtfeld bei Hastings" which treats the death of the Saxon king, but is narrower in scope than Tolstoy's.

6. Letter of May 5, 1869.

Chapter Five

1. I am following the traditional distribution of poems which had been made by Tolstoy and was followed in most subsequent editions of his work.

2. Arzamas. A literary society founded by Zhukovsky, Batyushkov, and Vyazemsky around 1815 which cultivated light poetry, and followed Karamzin's reform of literary Russian (which went in the direction of a more elegant French style, and the introduction of Gallicisms) in opposition to the "Archaists" who advocated the retention of Old Russian and Church Slavonic.

3. Among his European counterparts poets like Christian Morgenstern and Edward Lear could be mentioned.

4. Cf. the Soviet edition of Tolstoy's works, vol. 1, p. 771.

5. The poem may have been inspired by Heine's poem "Doch die Kastraten klagten."

6. The recent Soviet edition is also "expurgated."

7. It has been suggested that the poem referred to a concrete contemporary case, cf. Soviet edition of Tolstoy's works, vol. 1, p. 769.

8. M. Katkov, conservative editor of the *Russkii Vestnik;* V. Cherkassky, high government official in charge of internal Polish affairs; Y. Samarin, journalist and Slavophile theoretician.

9. Gostomysl was a legendary prince of Novgorod who allegedly invited the Varangians to come to Russia.

10. There is subtle allusion to the French revolutionists, the "sans-culottes" ("pantsless") in the poem, which makes Popov's "crime" appear more serious.

Chapter Six

1. Letter of October 1, 1856.
2. Letter to Markevich, March 20, 1860.
3. Cf. the poem "Where the clear spring" ("Gde svetlyi kliuch"), discussed in the chapter on lyric poetry.
4. Letter of November 17, 1856.
5. Letter of September 1867; italics in the original.

Chapter Seven

1. John was a fighter against the iconoclasts; cf. also the poem "Against the Current" ("Protiv techeniia").
2. Gavrila Derzhavin (1743-1816), greatest and most original Russian poet of the eighteenth century.
3. Letter to Princess Sayn-Wittgenstein, May 26, 1873.
4. A. A. Arakcheev (1769-1834), statesman under Paul I and Alexander I, known as an extreme reactionary who introduced an iron discipline in all departments subordinated to him.
5. Letter to Princess Sayn-Wittgenstein, May 7, 1875.

Chapter Eight

1. Johannes Fastenrath, "Vorwort zu Don Juan Tenorio von Don José Zorilla y Moral," Dresden, 1898, pp. LXX-LXXI. Zorilla's poem, written in 1844, was translated into German in 1850, and could have been known to Tolstoy.
2. The other two being Pushkin's "Kamenyi gost'," and N. Gumilev's "Don Zhuan v Egipte."
3. Tolstoy himself must have felt this, for in his letter to the editor of the *Russian Messenger* quoted above, he tried to point out the differences between his Don Juan and Faust.
4. Letter to Markevich, April 1, 1860.
5. All this had some parallels to the situation in Russia in the 1860's, and to Tolstoy's attitude to it; the poet actually used quotes from his *Don Juan* in a letter to Markevich (April 26, 1869) in which he argued with him about the "Polish question," that is, the forcible "Russification" of Poles which was undertaken by the Russian government.
6. Kurt Willimczik, *E. T. A. Hoffmann, Die drei Reiche seiner Gestaltwelt*, Inaugural Dissertation, Berlin, 1939, pp. 54-55.

7. Lorenzo Da Ponte, 1749-1838, Italian librettist and poet, commissioned by Mozart to write the librettos for *Le Nozze di Figaro*, *Don Giovanni*, and *Cosi Fan Tutte*.

Chapter Nine

1. D. S. Mirsky, *A History of Russian Literature*, London, 1949, p. 243.

2. Cf. Lirondelle, p. 397. It is interesting that both works appeared simultaneously in 1868.

3. Volume 3 of the Soviet edition, p. 454.

4. "Project for the Staging of the Tragedy *The Death of Ivan the Terrible*."

5. Later historians, such as Klyuchevsky, tend to question Godunov's guilt in Dmitry's murder.

6. In addition to it, Tolstoy used Kostomarov's *Smutnoe vremia moskovskogo gosudarstva v nachale 17. stoletiia*. Pogodin's *Istoriia v litsakh o tsare Borise Feodoroviche Godunove*. *Skazaniia kniazia Kurbskogo* (ed. by N. Ustryalov), *Zapiski gollandskogo kuptsa Isaaka Maasy*, etc.

7. Thus, e.g., in *The Death of Ivan the Terrible*, events are mentioned which occurred much earlier than 1584: the invasion of the Tatar khan occurred in 1572; Kurbsky's letter dates from 1579; the siege of Pskov under Shuysky's command took place in 1581; Ivan's murder of his son, his plan of abdication, the burning of the *Alexandrova sloboda* are events of 1582; Ivan's negotiations with the English ambassador took place in 1583. Similar anachronisms can be found in *Czar Fyodor* and *Czar Boris*.

8. Soviet edition of A. K. Tolstoy, volume 3, p. 457.

9. This feature is part of Tolstoy's reassessment and change of Godunov's character.

10. "Project for the Staging of *Czar Fyodor*." Count V. Sollogub objected to Fyodor's passive, yet crucial function and suggested that the intrigue revolve around Shuysky. However, Tolstoy refused to follow his advice, cf. *Vestnik Evropy*, 1908, letter to S. A. Tolstoy.

11. Letter to Markevich, December 13, 1868.

12. Letter to Princess Sayn-Wittgenstein, May 9, 1869.

13. "Project for the Staging of *Czar Fyodor*."

14. Acts 2, 3, and 4 should be dated, on one hand, 1602–the year of the arrival in Russia and death of the Danish prince; on the other hand, the events connected with Dmitry took place in 1604-5.

15. Letter to Karolina Pavlova, May 28, 1868; italics in the original.

16. Lirondelle, pp. 408-10.

17. E. L. Stahl, *Friedrich Schiller's Drama*, Oxford, 1954, p. 101.

18. The first scene of Act 1 (the dialogue between Saltykov and Voeykov) has its parallel in the first scene of Pushkin's drama (the dialogue between Vorotynsky and Shuysky); the scene in the house of Fyodor Nikitich Romanov (Act 3) when a toast is drunk to the czar, has a counterpart in the scene in Shuysky's house. And the scene with the people discussing Dmitry in Act 4 has also a parallel in the scene before the church.

19. Tolstoy used Karamzin, and Kostomarov's work *Severnorusskie narodopravstva vo vremena udel'no-vechevogo uklada*, St. Petersburg, 1863, for historical information.

20. Letter to Sof'ia Andreevna, August 3, 1870.

Selected Bibliography

PRIMARY SOURCES

Works by A. K. Tolstoy:

Polnoe sobranie sochinenii grafa A. K. Tolstogo, St. Petersburg, 1907, 4 vols.
Sobranie sochinenii v 4 tomakh, Moscow, 1963.
Stikhotvoreniia, Biblioteka poeta, ed. by I. Iampol'skii, Leningrad, 1936.
Dramaticheskaia trilogiia, ed. by I. Iampol'skii, Biblioteka poeta, Bol'shaia seriia, Leningrad, 1939.

Tolstoy's Works Translated into English:

Few of Tolstoy's works have been translated into English. Among those that have been are the following:

A Prince of Outlaws (Prince Serebryany), translated by Clarence A. Manning, New York, Alfred A. Knopf, 1927.
The Death of Ivan the Terrible, trans. by A. Hayes, London; K. Paul, Trench, Trubner, and Co., 1926.
Czar Fyodor, trans. by A. Hayes, London; K. Paul, Trench, Trubner, and Co., 1924.

SECONDARY SOURCES

AIKHENVAL'D, IU. *Siluety russkikh pisatelei,* M, 1909.
ANNENKOV, P. V. "Novaia istoricheskaia stsena," *Vestnik Evropy,* March, 1866.
BEGAK, B. and others. *Russkaia literaturnaia parodiia,* M-L, 1930.
BELETSKY, A. I. *Russkii romantizm,* sbornik statei, Academia, L, 1927.
BRODSKII, N. L. (ed.) *Literaturnye salony i kruzhki l. poloviny 19. veka,* M-L, 1930.
BEL'SKII, L. P. "Osnovnye motivy poezii grafa A. K. Tolstogo," *Russkoe obozrenie,* M, 1894, No. 3, pp. 378-93.
DAVYDOV, V. O. "Vospominaniia," *Russkii Arkhiv,* 1879, II, pp. 331ff.
DENISIUK, N. (ed.) *Kriticheskaia literatura o proizvedeniiakh grafa A. K. Tolstogo,* M, 1907.
FET, A. A. *Moi vospominaniia,* 1848-1889, M, 1890.
GNEDICH, P. P. *Kniga zhizni, Vospominaniia, 1885-1918, M,* 1929.
IUNGE, E. F. "Vospominaniia," *Vestnik Evropy,* 1905, vol. 2, p. 801.

KAMENSKAIA, M. F. "Vospominaniia," *Istoricheskii Vestnik,* 1909, CXV, pp. 134-37.

KNIAZEV, G. M. "Khomiakov i A. K. Tolstoi," *Russkii Vestnik,* 1901, vol. 276, No. 11, pp. 136-58; no. 12, pp. 515-30.

KONDRAT'EV, A. A. "K biografii A. K. Tolstogo," *Novyi put',* St. Petersburg, 1904, No. 1, pp. 181-208.

KOTLIAREVSKII, N. "Trilogiia grafa A. K. Tolstogo kak natsional'naia tragediia," *Vestnik Evropy,* Oct., 1902.

————. *Starinnye portrety,* St. Petersburg, 1907.

LEMKE, M. K., ed. *M. M. Stasiulevich i ego sovremenniki v ikh perepiske,* vols. 1-5, St. Petersburg, 1911-13.

LEVENSTIM, A. "A. K. Tolstoi," *Vestnik Evropy,* Oct., 1906, vol. 241, p. 487; vol. 242, p. 60.

LIRONDELLE, ANDRE. *Le Poète Alexis Tolstoi, L'homme et l'oeuvre.* Thèse pour le doctorat es lettres, Paris, 1912.

MESHCHERSKII, A. V. "Iz moei stariny," *Russkii Arkhiv,* 1900, No. 7, p. 373.

MIRSKY, D. S. *A History of Russian Literature,* London, 1949.

NIKITIN, A. "Graf A. K. Tolstoi v literature 60-kh godov," *Russkii Vestnik,* 1894, No. 2, pp. 303-20.

POKROVSKII, V. I. (ed.) *Aleksei Konstantinovich Tolstoi, Ego zhizn' i sochineniia,* M, 1909.

SALOMON, M. "Don Zhuan grafa A. K. Tolstogo," *Vestnik Evropy,* 1907, vol. 247, pp. 483 ff.

SOLLOGUB, V. *Vospiminaniia,* St. Petersburg, 1887.

SOLOV'EV, V. S. "Poeziia A. K. Tolstogo," *Vestnik Evropy,* 1895, vol. 3, pp. 237 ff.

————. Preface to "The Vampire" by A. K. Tolstoy, St. Petersburg, 1900.

STAFEEV, G. I. *A. K. Tolstoj, Bibliograficheskij ukazatel',* Brjansk, 1969.

TSERTELEV, D. N. "Dramaticheskaia trilogiia A. K. Tolstogo," *Russkii Vestnik,* 1899, vol. 263, No. 10, pp. 652-72; 1900, vol. 270, No. 11, pp. 187, ff.

————. "Graf A. K. Tolstoi v ego stikhotvoreniiakh," *Russkii Vestnik,* 1900, no. 11.

VIAZEMSKII, P. A. "Vospominaniia," in *Polnoe sobranie sochinenii,* St. Petersburg, 1878-96, vol. VIII, p. 413.

ZAMOTIN, I. I. *Sorokovye i shestidesiatye gody. Ocherki po istorii russkoi literatury 19. stoletiia.* Petrograd, 1915.

ZHEMCHUZHNIKOV, L. M. "Otryvki iz moikh vospominanii," *Vestnik Evropy,* 1899, pp. 230 ff.

ZHEMCHUZHNIKOV, V. M. "Zapiski," *Vestnik Evropy,* February, 1899, vol. 2, pp. 634-65.

Index

(The works of A. K. Tolstoy are listed under his name.)

173

Index 181